ZAKK WYLDE

By Toby Wine

Guitar: Doug Boduch
Bass: Tom McGir
Drums: Scott Schroedl
Keyboards: Warren Wiegratz
Recording and Mixing Engineer: Jim Reith

Cover photo by Neil Zlozower

Cherry Lane Music Company
Educational Director/Project Supervisor: Susan Poliniak
Director of Publications: Mark Phillips

ISBN 1-57560-727-1

Visit our website at www.cherrylane.com

Table of Contents

The Zakk Wylde Story: Oh, The Brewtality! 4

A Selected Discography 5

Zakk's Equipment 6

About the Author 7

Acknowledgments 7

Miracle Man 8

No More Tears 13

Horse Called War 17

Perry Mason 21

1,000,000 Miles Away 26

Born to Lose 31

Counterfeit God 35

All for You 39

Speedball 42

The Blessed Hellride 47

Suffering Overdue 51

Stillborn 57

Guitar Notation Legend 62

The Zakk Wylde Story: Oh, The Brewtality!

You like heavy metal? Zakk Wylde *is* heavy metal. With his chiseled physique, flowing blond mane, and intimidating, Hell's Angel's–style beard, Zakk is a rock star of the old school. His image and music hearken back to the days when heavy metal was the province of scowling toughs in beat-up leather and denim, "men's men" who pounded out bruising riffs on Les Pauls and flying Vs. Hairspray and leopard-print spandex were the uniforms of streetwalkers, not musicians, and six-foot-high, stacks of rack-mounted digital processors stayed in the studios where they belonged. Zakk is a defender of the faith and an enemy of the poseur, the genuine article in an era of phonies and plastic pop stars. But he didn't just spring from the womb with massive biceps and chops to match—he evolved.

Born on January 14th, 1967, in Jersey City, New Jersey, Zakk was a typical kid with two loving parents and a passion for athletics. Although he failed to make his high school football team, he remains a dedicated fan of the New York Yankees and the NFL's New York Giants. As anyone who is familiar with New Jersey can attest, there's never a shortage of fledgling guitar heroes lurking around the bend, and one of them, Leroy Wright, happened to be the coach's son. Zakk was blown away by his skill with a Les Paul and became an instant convert and dedicated student of Wright's over the next two years. Zakk threw himself into the woodshed and practiced with abandon, developing the basis of a prodigious technique and soon gaining entry to the local fraternity of six-string gunslingers. His new pals turned him onto jazz fusion virtuosos like Al Di Meola and John McLaughlin, sparking Zakk's interest in theory and scale-based improvisation, while his teacher put him to work on classical guitar to fulfill his desire for ever more challenging material.

Like many a teenage guitarist, Zakk soon found himself engrossed in the one-upmanship and ego clashes of the local music store. The competitive environment both helped and hurt him, for while it provided a daily yardstick by which he could gauge his progress, there was a distinct lack of encouragement for young players to discover the soulful side of music. He had a revelation during a jam session in which he was flying through his scales while soloing on the Doobie Brothers' "Listen to the Music." By his own admission, his playing was "awful," and he realized he didn't know a thing about playing the blues—the foundation of rock 'n' roll soloing. So began a new course of study, highlighted by his examination of the work of Alvin Lee (who he has called "the Yngwie of 1969") and informal work under Dave DiPietro of Jersey club legends T.T. Quick. DiPietro encouraged Zakk to take his time developing a solo and schooled him in the expressive arts of string bending and vibrato. Today, even a cursory listen to Zakk's recorded output confirms the depth of his blues influences and his maturation into a virtuoso player whose quicksilver runs ooze with blues feeling.

Zakk spent his teenage years in a steadily revolving carousel of bands, beginning with his first group, Stone Henge, which he assembled in 1984. He'd become a regular on the New Jersey club circuit by the time he was approached by a photographer's assistant who'd recently made a passing acquaintance with Ozzy Osbourne. Both he and Zakk were aware of the bandleader's need for a new guitarist, and the man promised that a demo tape would make it into Ozzy's hands. Wylde whipped one up the next day, the man proved true to his word, and in what must have seemed like a dream shockingly come true, he was soon firmly ensconced as the legend's newest guitar hero. From the beginning, it was a match made in heavy metal heaven, as Ozzy assumed a warmly paternal role with the young whiz kid. Zakk in turn helped fill the void of musical and emotional camaraderie that had been gaping since the untimely demise of the youthful icon Randy Rhoads (one of Zakk's key influences). Osbourne had always maintained a close partnership with his guitarists, from Black Sabbath's Tony Iommi, to Rhoads and tasty players like Jake E. Lee and Brad Gillis. He'd found his newest right-hand man in an oddball coincidence of time and place. Zakk was 19 years old.

It was during his long stint with Ozzy that Zakk began his ascent towards his current status as one of rock's most important and terrifying guitarists. On a steady stream of blockbuster tours and albums (beginning with 1988's *No Rest for the Wicked*) Zakk proved himself a captivating soloist capable of moments of jaw-dropping pyrotechnics and a formidable composer of memorable melodies and bone-crushing riffs. Taking center stage in what is arguably the most visible guitar spot in the world of heavy rock, Wylde developed a legion of dedicated fans enthralled by his fretboard prowess and screaming artificial harmonics. When Ozzy began a short-lived retirement following 1992's *No More Tears* tour, Zakk kept busy with a new power trio, Pride & Glory, whose eponymous debut was released in 1994. It revealed a side of Zakk's musicality that had been hidden in Osbourne's ensemble. The songs touched upon a variety of styles, showcased Wylde's love of Skynyrd-inspired Southern rock, and found him covering the vocal duties for the first time. Before long, however, his bandmates went their separate ways, Ozzy was itching to get back to work, and Zakk returned to the fold for 1995's *Ozzmosis* and its subsequent world tour.

1996 was a slower year for Osbourne and company, allowing Zakk to work on his debut solo album, *Book of Shadows*. The record sold modestly but surprised and impressed both listeners and critics with its versatility and gentler tone. With the reunion of the iconic supergroup Black Sabbath in 1998, Ozzy's regular working band was put on hiatus, and Zakk quickly got back to work on his own projects. He formed the Black Label Society and released the highly anticipated *Sonic Brew* in 1999. Fans were not disappointed, as it was clear from the album's opening moments that BLS would be a no-nonsense metal juggernaut of unrelenting power. On follow-up albums like *Stronger than Death*, *Alcohol Fueled Brewtality Live*, *1919 Eternal*, and *The Blessed Hellride*, the band cemented their reputation as today's foremost practitioners of ultra-heavy, take-no-prisoners metal. With bad attitudes and a tremendous quantity of beer, BLS creates drop-tuned, riff-based songs in the spirit of the music's golden age, when men were men and eardrums bled. A generation of fans were given the antidote for 20 years of glam rock, hair metal, and the grungy, Seattle-style garage bands of the '90s. The Black Label Society released *Hangover Music Vol. VI*, on April 20, 2004; it sold over 10,000 copies on the first day and continues to confound the naysayers with both its artistic and commercial success.

Today, Zakk lives in L.A. and tries to keep a low profile when he isn't on the road. He's a dedicated body builder, and his manic energy and metabolism—which one suspects is cranked up to a level that would be deadly for the average citizen—keeps him ticking when the rest of us would be passed out from sheer exhaustion. But at home, he's a family man who loves his wife and kids, playing his guitars, and hanging out with his rottweilers. He once called himself "the Al Bundy of metal." His unpretentious, utterly-incapable-of-bull personality ruffles a lot of feathers. He scorns the rock star life and hides a thoughtful, serious side—especially when it comes to music—with a steady stream of wisecracks and self-effacing humor. Zakk loves metal, steaks, microbrews, and motorcycles; digs the Allman Brothers, Van Halen, and Elton John; and lists his father and Ozzy as his idols and role models.

A Selected Discography

Solo:
Book of Shadows (1996)

Pride & Glory:
Pride & Glory (1994)

Black Label Society:
Sonic Brew (1999)
Stronger than Death (2000)
Alcohol Fueled Brewtality Live (2001)
1919 Eternal (2002)
The Blessed Hellride (2003)
Hangover Music Vol. VI (2004)

Ozzy Osbourne:
No Rest for the Wicked (1988)
Just Say Ozzy (1989)
No More Tears (1991)
Mama I'm Coming Home (1992)
Live & Loud (1993)
Ozzmosis (1995)
Down to Earth (2001)
Live at Budokan (2002)

With Others:
Bill Ward—*Ward One: Along the Way* (1989)
CPR—*Coven/Pitrelli/Reilly* (1992)
L.A. Blues Authority—*L.A. Blues Authority* (1992)
Black Sabbath—*Under Wheels of Confusion 1970–1987* (1996)
Carmine Appice—*Channel Mind Radio: Guitar Zeus, Vol. 2* (1997)
Various Artists—*Merry Axemas, Vol. 2: More Guitars for Christmas* (1998; Zakk performs "White Christmas")
Various Artists—*Humanary Stew: A Tribute to Alice Cooper* (1999)
Rock Star—*Original Movie Soundtrack* (2001)
Derek Sherinian—*Inertia* (2001)
Derek Sherinian—*Black Utopia* (2003)

Zakk's Equipment

Guitars

Zakk carries up to seven different Gibson Les Pauls on the road, but generally uses only three on each gig. His preference is for his signature model with its trademark black and white bull's-eye (a replica of his original, a gift from his parents) or his "rebel" guitar with the bottle cap paint job. Zakk has two Gibson 1275 double necks, one of which is used during Ozzy's encore, "Momma I'm Coming Home." He also owns a '57 Black Beauty Les Paul with silver-mirrored inlay and an SG which was used to record "1,000,000 Miles Away." Wylde uses a custom string set of GHS Boomers in gauges .010, .013, .016, .036, .052, and .060 or .070, depending on how far down the low E string will be tuned (anywhere from a half step to a full 6th below standard tuning!). Zakk's main axes are equipped with EMG active electronics 81 and 85 pickups. He also owns a banjo and a number of steel- and nylon-string acoustic guitars, including a favorite Alvarez Yari model setup to mimic the playability of his Les Pauls. Zakk never uses a vibrato bar.

Amplifiers

Zakk uses Marshall JCM800s, with the stock power tubes replaced with 6550s. His cabinets have had their Celestion speakers replaced with 200-watt EV speakers for punch and clarity. The preamp volume controls are always set at ten, with the master volumes at four and six, and the cabinets are miked on each side with Shure SM57 and Audio Technica AT4060 microphones.

Effects

Zakk employs a Dunlop Jimi Hendrix Wah Pedal (he uses this more as a treble boost than anything else, especially for pick harmonics), a Dunlop Rotovibe (used only occasionally, and only in its green chorus stage), a Boss SD1 Super Overdrive pedal, and a Boss CE-2 Chorus Ensemble pedal. Zakk has given up on his wireless system because of its tendency to inhibit feedback (which he employs to great effect), so his 30-foot cable runs directly to the wah pedal. The Boss stomp box has two outputs, which allow Zakk's guitar tech, Sean Paden, to split the signal and run it in stereo to his amps; each of the overdrive pedal's three controls are set at two o'clock, and Wylde turns it off and rolls his guitar's volume knob down for quieter songs and sections.

Beer

These include an assortment of craft- and micro-brewed beers from around the world. As of this writing, one of his favorites is California's delicious Sierra Nevada, which comes in pale ale, porter, stout, and seasonal varieties. Zakk eschews America's watered-down, mass-produced commercial beers and has expressed great surprise to find young Britons drinking these brands in England, where products such as Samuel Smith's Oatmeal Stout and Young's Ramrod are freely and cheaply available. He's also teaching himself the art of homebrewing and hopes to produce his own Black Label Society beers in the near future, aspiring to one day unleash varieties like Blood Red, Liver Launcher, and Kidney Crusher on the world.

About the Author

Toby Wine was born and raised in New York City and spent the weekends of his adolescence in clubs like CBGB's, L'amour's, the Ritz, and Irving Plaza, faithfully attending the performances of such bands as Slayer, Metallica, the Cro-Mags, Agnostic Front, D.R.I., and Anthrax. A regular contributor to the many fanzines covering the underground metal and hardcore scene, Toby also led his own trio, Infantile Disorder, and traded tapes and correspondence with like-minded musicians from across the U.S. and Europe. He later earned a degree in composition from the Manhattan School of Music and has had his songs and arrangements recorded by various jazz artists for labels including Steeplechase, Muse, Sharp Nine, and K-Pasta. He's worked as a score preparer for avant-garde jazz legend Ornette Coleman, and as the music librarian for the Carnegie Hall Jazz Band. Today, Toby gigs frequently around the tri-state area, teaches privately, and works as a freelance writer, editor, studio guitarist, and arranger. Some of his many Cherry Lane titles include *The Art of Texas Blues*, *Steely Dan Legendary Licks*, *1001 Blues Licks*, and *Metallica Under the Microscope*. He can be reached by email at: tobywine@ez2www.com.

Acknowledgments

I'd like to express my gratitude to Susan Poliniak, Mark Phillips, and the entire Cherry Lane family, and to give thanks to my parents, Rosemary and Jerry, and to Jack, Bibi, Bob, Noah, and Sam. Thanks to all for your ongoing patience, understanding, and expert advice. Additional thanks and credit go to all the friends who've stood by me and to all the teachers who taught me what little I know about playing music and writing words.

TRACK 01

Note: Track 1 contains tuning pitches.

Miracle Man

from **No Rest for the Wicked (1988)**

Words and Music by
Ozzy Osbourne, Zakk Wylde and Bob Daisley

Like Zakk Wylde, Ozzy Osbourne is a man that is easily misunderstood. Both have their moments of over-the-top, rock-star showmanship, but each is a skilled musician and dedicated family man. Ozzy in particular has been forced to defend his music and character for decades from attack by organizations such as the Parents Music Resource Center (with Tipper Gore leading the charge) and conservative Christian groups led by televangelist Jimmy Swaggart, in whose direction "Miracle Man" is most pointedly directed.

Perhaps Ozzy was tired of being lambasted for songs like "Suicide Solution," written and recorded with the late Randy Rhoads. The message of that song was crystal clear to anyone with a sixth-grade education—alcohol abuse will eventually kill you—and it was presented by a man and in a way that would reach young listeners far more effectively than the uncomprehending Reagans telling them to "just say no." When Zakk came up with the riff for "Miracle Man" shortly after joining the band, Ozzy had the perfect platform to take a well-deserved lyrical swipe at the man who'd been a thorn in his side for years. Maybe he figured that if Swaggart couldn't discern the irony in "Suicide Solution" (he probably never even heard the song), he'd interpret "Miracle Man" as genuine praise!

Verse Riff

This riff, a simplification of the song's Intro, coincides with Ozzy's vocal entrance. Remember to tune each of your guitar's strings down a half step if you're planning to play along with the recording. Begin the riff with your 3rd finger on the 2nd fret of the A string, allowing you to slide to the 4th fret for the F#5 chord while your index finger hammers on from the open low E string to its 2nd fret. Create the artificial harmonics in the third and fourth measures of the example by striking the string with your pick and a bit of thumb or index fingertip at the same time. (Artificial harmonics take a bit of practice and are always easier with a heavily overdriven tone.) Try using an upstroke for these double stops to ensure that the higher string is pinched, creating the harmonic. Note that the first should sound an octave higher than the fretted B, while the second should sound a 10th above (D#). Vary the location of your pick attack between the end of your guitar's fretboard and bridge to change the pitch of the harmonic. Generally speaking, playing above the neck pickup will produce an octave, while picking directly in the center between the two pickups should result in a high D#.

TRACK 02

Tune down 1/2 step:
(low to high) E♭–A♭–D♭–G♭–B♭–E♭

Moderate Rock ♩ = 138

E5 F#5

P.M. -

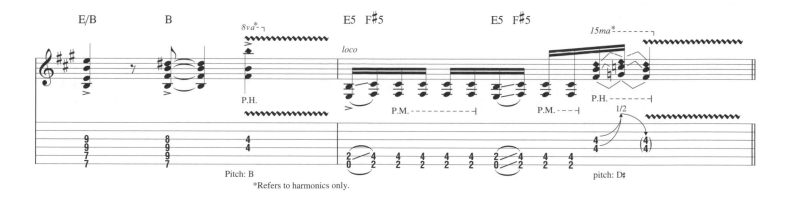

Pre-Chorus

Begin this section by sliding up the neck from the opening C#5 chord to a half step double bend on the B and G strings played with an index-finger barre. While this riff is highly typical of Zakk's work with Ozzy, mixing as it does power chords and "special effects" such as bends and vibrato, the phrase is broken up in the fourth measure by a neat little ringing passage played on the B, G, and D strings. Use your index finger to barre the strings across the 4th fret while snagging the E at the B string's 5th fret with your middle finger. The example wraps up with a series of descending, palm-muted power chords; be sure to use steady alternate picking while letting the side of your picking hand rest lightly on the strings where they meet the bridge to muffle them appropriately.

TRACK 03

Chorus

This slick little riff was the seed from which the entire "Miracle Man" composition was born; like many memorable songs, the hook came first, and then the Verses and the other sections that are a natural outgrowth of the Chorus were developed later. Begin by hammering on with your index finger to the 2nd fret of the low E string, and then use your pinky to barre the top two strings at the 5th fret. If you leave your first finger in place, it can serve to mute the open A, D, and G strings. Finish the opening measure with ring- and index-finger barres on the D and G strings' 4th and 2nd frets, respectively, before quickly shifting to get to the final eighth note double stop with your index and middle fingers. The example below shows the song's second Chorus, which ends with the stop-time "hits" in the final two measures, setting up Zakk's solo. Only the last of the four 16th note pairs is palm-muted, but you should employ the mute *after* each of the first three to avoid feedback, buzzing, and/or the jangle of open strings.

TRACK 04

Solo

As you'll see as you work your way through this book, the free-spirited and reckless Zakk Wylde, who has described his style as "pentatonic scales on beer and steroids," is actually a pretty thoughtful musician with a strong grasp of his art's most essential elements: melody, harmony, rhythm, and timbre. In his "Miracle Man" Solo, he proceeds in a fiery but logical fashion, executing cleanly with rhythmic precision and a thick, unadulterated tone that slices neatly through a very loud, bottom-heavy ensemble. It's not uncommon to hear a hard rock band in live performance and have difficulty discerning the actual *notes* that the guitarist plays in his Solo—they're so awash in distortion and other effects that the original attack has long since disappeared. Fans of Zakk Wylde don't have this problem, as he refuses to clutter up his Les Paul/Marshall stack tone with extraneous processing.

Zakk begins this Solo with a series of three-note arpeggios played in an even 16th note rhythm, so that the lowest note falls only on the first and fourth beats of each measure. The arpeggios outline an F# suspended chord (in inversion), a C# minor triad (superimposed over E5), and a D major triad. Use your middle finger on the B string, and your index and pinky fingers on the high E string for each. In the fourth measure, he reverses suit, outlining an F# suspended chord in a descending four-note arpeggio fit into a sextuplet rhythm! It's an ingenious and highly sophisticated phrase, and it's repeated after the very widely vibratoed B at the end of the fourth measure. Things move in a different direction in measure 8 (watch out for those 2/4 bars!), with a series of wah-inflected bends, a longer, held bend picked in a quarter note triplet rhythm, and a truly wild bend up two whole steps at the end of measure 13. After a series of ascending unison bends (the G string is pushed up a whole step with the ring finger to match the pitch on the B string), Zakk tops the Solo off with a heavily vibratoed B string bend that he strikes at random intervals to ensure sustain over a full four measures.

TRACK 05

TRACK 06
Slow Demo

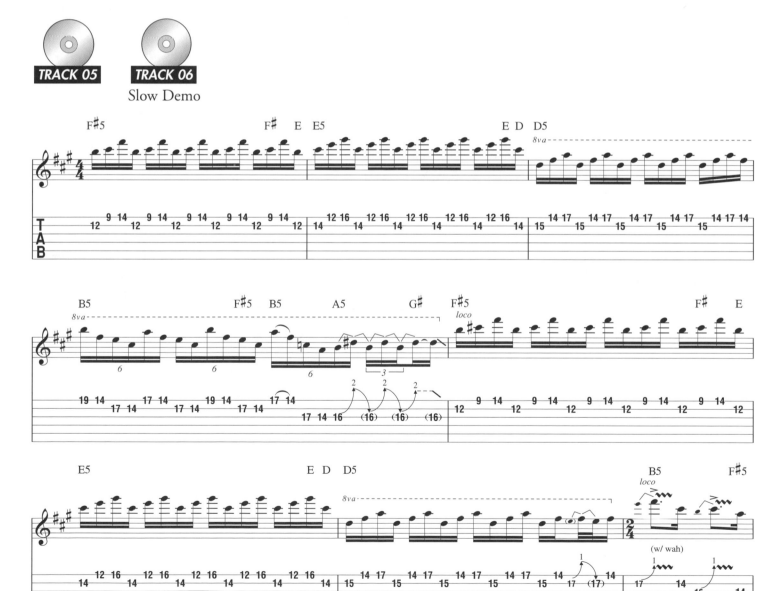

Miracle Man Cont.

No More Tears

from *No More Tears (1991)*

Words and Music by
Ozzy Osbourne, Zakk Wylde, Randy Castillo, Michael
Inez and John Purdell

With its strings, synths, and long instrumental Interlude, "No More Tears" is a far cry from Ozzy's more Black Sabbath–flavored music, but its Verse in particular retains the slow, grinding heaviness fans have come to expect from the grand old man of heavy metal. This heaviness is reinforced by an unusual guitar tuning Zakk Wylde often employs when playing with the wizard of Oz—drop D tuning, and then all six strings lowered a half step, resulting in D♭–A♭–D♭–G♭–B♭–E♭, low to high. The other, more elaborate arranging and orchestrational trappings of the song may reflect a taste of Ozzy's broader musical sensibility. Whether it's the native English music he heard as a child, Tony Iommi's passion for jazz guitarist Wes Montgomery, Randy Rhoads' classical guitar work, or Zakk Wylde's love of the Allman Brothers, Osbourne has well over three decades of influencing and being influenced behind him. Some sounds may be co-opted, while others are rejected out of hand, but any artist must be allowed to change and grow, lest he risk stagnation. The fans may not always love the results, but Ozzy's track record is one of remarkable and consistent success.

Verse Riff

Zakk Wylde, a long time fan of Southern rock and blues, employs a bottleneck slide throughout "No More Tears." The song couldn't sound less like Lynyrd Skynyrd, but Zakk proves definitively that a slide can be an effective tool in a metal guitarist's arsenal. If you're unfamiliar with this very cool technique, this is a good time to start learning! Try wearing the slide on your pinky so your other three fingers can fret notes in the usual fashion. The slide should be placed lightly on the string (don't press down) directly above the fret wire, rather than above the wood of the fretboard. If you want to play the E at the 12th fret of the low E string, place the slide above the metal between the 12th and 13th frets. Generally speaking, the higher your action is, the easier the slide will be to use. This isn't a technique you can learn overnight—it will require patient practice to gain facility and, more importantly, the ability to play *in tune*. Be sure to keep the slide perfectly parallel with the frets, and lay your index finger gently across the strings behind the slide to eliminate any unwanted whines or vibrations.

In the first half of the riff below, keep the slide out of the way and use your index, middle, and ring fingers on the 4th, 5th, and 6th frets, respectively. The phrase ends with one of Zakk's trademark artificial harmonics, which he bends up a whole step, adorning it with heavy vibrato, really making it squeal. The second half of the riff incorporates the slide. Listen carefully to the way Wylde phrases here—he's sliding around, but it's controlled and never exaggerated. Use a light touch throughout, especially on the 10th fret barre that alternates with the open D and G strings. You don't want to slap the slide down onto the neck.

TRACK 07

Tune down 1/2 step:
(low to high) D♭–A♭–D♭–G♭–B♭–E♭

Moderate Rock ♩ = 100

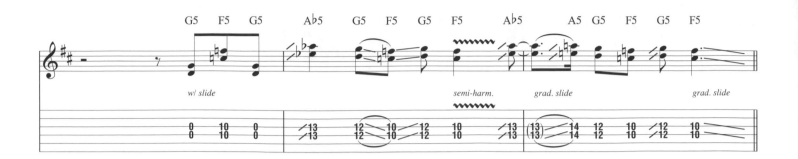

Pre-Chorus

This straightforward section is complicated somewhat by the presence of the slide on the little finger, a necessity towards the end of the phrase. The excerpt below shows only the second half of the Pre-Chorus, as its first four measures are nearly identical to the first four shown here. Things begin easily enough, with an open string D5 chord and a bit of crunchy palm-muted playing. Fret the E5/D, Dm7, and B♭5 chords with your index and ring fingers while your pinky holds the slide away from the neck. The phrase ends with a series of sliding chords and double stops—time the first ascent so you arrive at the E5 chord precisely on the downbeat of the fifth measure, then follow suit with the ascent to F5 and the climb back down the neck to the Chorus.

TRACK 08

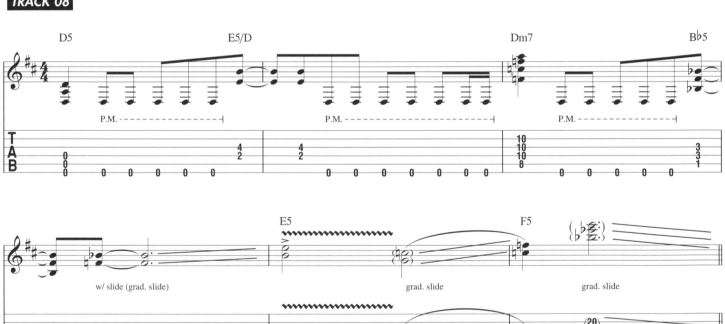

Chorus Riff

This section is a simple two-measure phrase that's repeated four times. The only (somewhat) tricky part here is shifting cleanly from the long, sliding descent that ends the previous section to the fretted notes shown here. Try not to lift the slide away from the neck too soon! Execute the first grace note slide up to D with your index finger, and then play the higher D and C on the G string with your ring and middle fingers, respectively. Shift quickly to play the third low D with your middle finger, using your index finger to play the Bb that follows. The four power chords that end the phrase should be played with your index, middle, and ring fingers barring the two lowest strings at the 3rd, 5th, and 6th frets.

TRACK 09

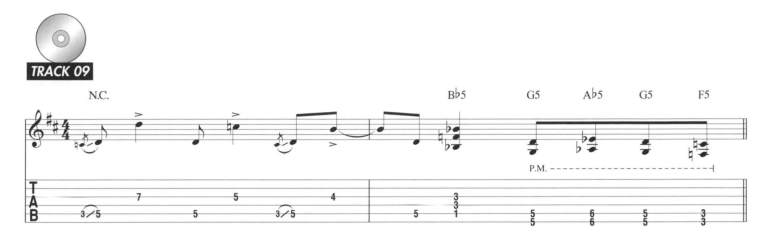

Solo

This smoldering statement begins after the long piano-and-strings Interlude and brings us back into the realm of the headbanger with a vengeance. Zakk leads up to the Solo with some anticipatory bends (not shown here), and then takes center stage, once again displaying his extraordinary rhythmic sensibility. Don't content yourself with merely learning the notes in the licks—these are musical *phrases* and should be approached as such. Zakk is clearly aware of his place within an ensemble—he's not just throwing out all his tricks with a deaf ear turned towards his bandmates. The Solo includes a number of blues-drenched licks based on notes from the D blues scale (D–F–G–Ab–A–C) and D Dorian mode (D–E–F–G–A–B–C), but it also includes a few F#s that suggest D Mixolydian (D–E–F#–G–A–B–C). Zakk also throws in a handful of tasty double stops on the B and G strings while staying in 10th position for the first four measures. He moves up the neck and continues his bluesy wailing in measures 5 and 6, and then finishes the Solo with a four-measure phrase that's pure heavy metal. Use your index and ring fingers throughout the first three measures of this lick (all sextuplets) and watch how slickly Zakk changes positions with the smooth B string slide at the end of the first measure. As he accelerates towards the Solo's climax, he spits out 32nd notes that follow the ascending chords, outlining inverted Bb and C major triads. You'll need to use your pinky here to pull-off to your index finger, while getting to the notes on the B string with your middle finger. When you've put all of the elements together and slowly worked the Solo up to speed, try playing along with the recording and see if you can match Zakk note for note!

TRACK 10   **TRACK 11**
Slow Demo

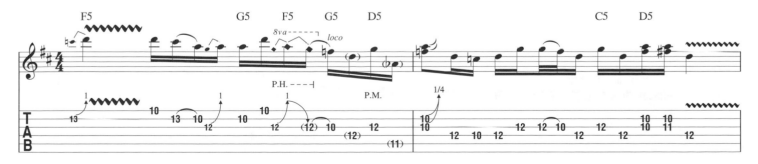

No More Tears Cont.

Horse Called War

from *Pride & Glory (1994)*

Words and Music by
Zakk Wylde

Pride & Glory was the name of both Zakk's power trio featuring James LoMenzo (bass) and Brian Tichy (drums), and the sole album they released on Geffen records. P & G afforded Wylde the room he needed to record songs that didn't quite fit the bill with Ozzy, and to explore his love of Southern rock (he even gets out his trusty banjo on a few numbers!). "Horse Called War" is a more straight-ahead affair, an all-out embrace of noisy, blues-inflected metal inspired in part by a song by, of all people, Janis Joplin. "Move Over" featured the late singer doubling its instrumental riff with her voice, an approach that Zakk echoes here in the song's Verse sections.

Main Riff

After a cacophonous Introduction, P & G settle into this chunky little riff that creates an "over the barline" feeling by dividing the 16 eighth notes in every two measures into six–six–four groupings. The unmuted power chords give the riff its contour and serve as accents that divide the groups of eighth notes across the measures of the phrase. Play the three-note chords in the second measure—inverted D and C triads—with ring- and index-finger barres, respectively.

TRACK 12

Verse Lick

Here's the line that doubles Zakk's vocal melody; each time we hear this phrase, it's followed by a four-measure return to the song's main riff. Taken directly from the A blues scale (A–C–D–E♭–E–G), the fourth measure departs harmonically with descending double stops on the A and D strings that imply E7, E♭7, and D7 chords. The lick begins with one of Zakk's trademark pick (or "pinch") harmonics; your fretting hand should play the note in the normal way, while your picking hand creates a pitch an octave above by adding the edge of the thumb or index fingertip to your usual pick attack. If you're not familiar with this technique, you will be by the time you get through with this book—it pops up everywhere. Be patient and experiment with pick attack and finger placement to discover the best ways for *you* to create these very cool effects. You'll find that the more cranked up your amp and the more distortion-saturated your tone, the easier it is produce these "artificial harmonics." Also, try altering the distance from the guitar's bridge that you "pinch"—you'll be able to get a variety of harmonic tones by moving forwards or backwards.

Chorus

Zakk's simple arpeggios here allow bassist James LoMenzo to get busy, as the greatly reduced density of the guitar part leaves room for more action, both rhythmically and melodically, in the lower register. The A minor progression descends in a familiar pattern for three measures before rising again with some chunky E5 and G5 power chords. Use your index finger on the B string and middle finger on the G string; they can remain in place in the third measure if you reach around the top of your guitar's neck to grab the low F with your thumb.

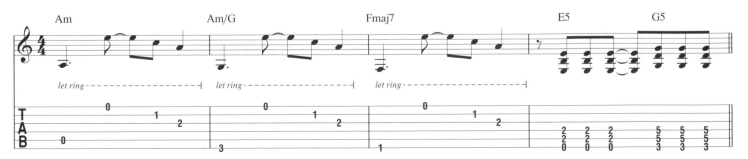

Solo

This is a typical Zakk Wylde solo in that it's filled with fiery licks and tricks and exudes his hell-bent attitude without ever flying completely out of control. Zakk stays in position for the majority of the Solo, playing from the A minor pentatonic scale (A–C–D–E–G) in 5th position for the Solo's first four measures, then rising to 7th position to play from the B minor pentatonic scale (B–D–E–F♯–A) for the next eight, and 9th position to access the C♯ pentatonic minor scale (C♯–E–F♯–G♯–B) for another eight measures. Don't miss his killer "racecar" effect in measures 6, 7, and 8, in which he strikes the top three strings then flicks his toggle switch back and forth between the bridge and neck pickups (with the volume knob for the neck pick up rolled off completely) in an accelerating triplet rhythm—it really sounds like traffic speeding on by and into the distance! The Solo's final nine measures feature a series of unison bends that rise along the B and G strings as the (implied) harmony moves down. The first of the two unison bends are tremolo picked—they should be picked up and down as fast as possible in no specific rhythm except that which is indicated in the notation (this is a technique often employed by mandolin players in Greek and Italian bands). Zakk plays an unusual lick in the fourth and fifth measures from the end in which the notes E and D♯ are repeated while he shifts between G and A above. The Solo then wraps up with a long, very wide bend (up two whole steps!) on the low E string.

TRACK 15

TRACK 16
Slow Demo

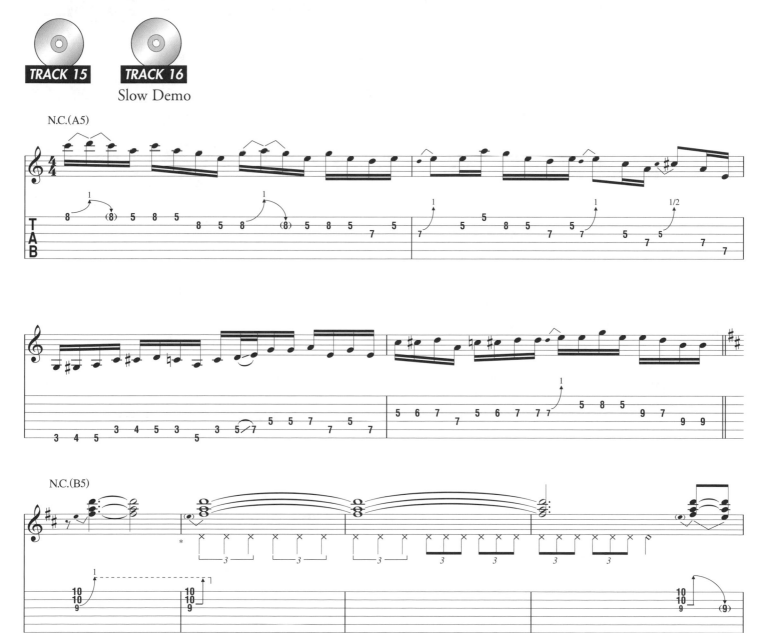

*Flick toggle switch btwn. on & off positions in rhythm indicated.

19

Perry Mason

from *Ozzmosis (1995)*

Words and Music by
Ozzy Osbourne, Zakk Wylde and John Purdell

One gets the sense that there may be just a *wee* touch of irony in Ozzy's very popular song "Perry Mason," inspired by the character (created by Erle Stanley Gardner and famously portrayed by Raymond Burr) and TV show of the same name. The lyric "someone to put you in place" sounds sarcastic and not very laudatory, but Ozzy may well be a huge fan. "Perry Mason" features a catchy Chorus melody and prominent synthesizers, but has enough churning guitar riffs and licks to keep the diehards happy, too. Don't forget to tune down for this one: Zakk begins by dropping the low E string down a whole step to D, and then brings all six strings down a half step further, leaving you with Db–Ab–Db–Gb–Bb–Eb (low to high).

Intro and Chorus Licks

"Perry Mason" begins with a dramatic chordal passage followed by synthesizers that introduce a pulsing riff that seems closer to a techno/house mix than anything Ozzy ever did. After a series of bone-crunching power chord "hits," Zakk enters in earnest with a part that combines melodic unison bends with chords and artificial harmonics that also serves as the underlying accompaniment to Ozzy's vocals in the song's Chorus. Take note that "Perry Mason" is played in 12/8, rather than the usual 4/4 time signature used in the great majority of rock songs. As is often the case elsewhere, the 12/8 groove here feels very much like a slow 4/4 in which each beat is divided into three equal pieces (i.e., a triplet). It's best to try and "feel" the song (and tap your foot) on the 1st, 4th, 7th, and 10th eighth notes in each measure, breaking the groove down into a slow, loping 4/4 feel. Also, remember to make the requisite adjustments while reading the notated music—if an eighth note gets one beat in 12/8, then there are two (not four) 16th notes per beat, four dotted quarter notes per measure, etc.

The licks in this section aren't too difficult in and of themselves; the five unison bends along the B and G strings that start the phrase should be played with your index and ring fingers, the latter pushing the G string up a whole step to match the pitch on the B string above. After that, it's a series of sustained chords and the special effects that are staples of Zakk's repertoire. Make sure you crank the distortion to get those artificial harmonics really squealing, and then shake the hell out of 'em. Make your pick scrapes roar like a jet engine passing overhead.

TRACK 17

Drop D tuning, down 1/2 step:
(low to high) Db–Ab–Db–Gb–Bb–Eb

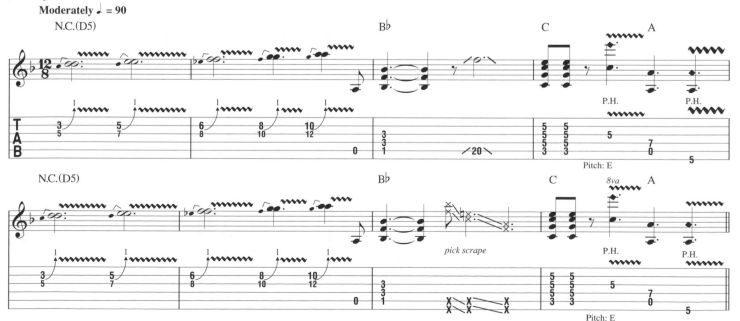

Verse Riff

Play the D octaves that begin this phrase with your index finger on the G string, flattened slightly to muffle the open B string, and with your pinky on the high E string. Try beginning with a downstroke and use alternate picking throughout. This is a deceptively tricky riff to play cleanly, so as you're learning it make sure you really slow it down and then slowly bring it back up to tempo with no loss of precision. Each of the three-note power chords here (the lowest note is doubled an octave higher) should be played with a barre—use your index finger for the F5 and G5 chords that slide from the 3rd to the 5th fret.

TRACK 18

Pre-Chorus

This section is quite complex rhythmically and teeters over the barline on a number of occasions, so be sure you know on which beat each element falls (don't be afraid to count!). Begin by playing the G5 chords with a ring-finger barre; use the same finger, backed up by the index and middle fingers, to perform the step-and-a-half low E string bend in measure 3. There's another one of Zakk's trademark screaming harmonics in the penultimate measure, and then a series of chromatic power chords in the last—stay in 3rd position here, so that your ring finger barres the 3rd fret, your middle finger barres the 4th, and so on.

TRACK 19

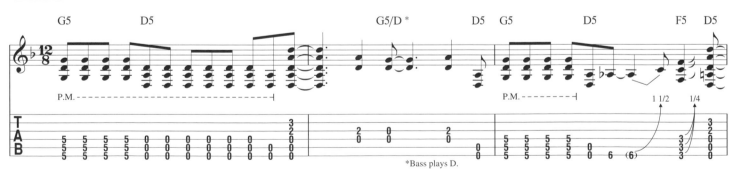

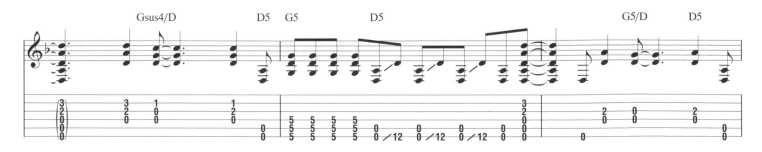

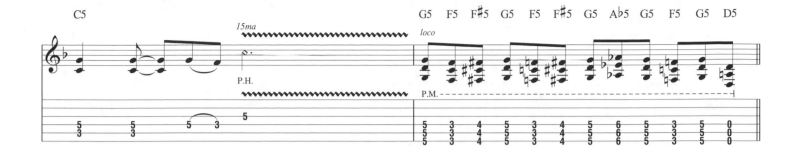

Solo

This 16-measure outing is Zakk Wylde in a nutshell—virtuosic, lightning-quick, rhythmically and melodically adventurous, and filled with beautiful and lyrical moments and a healthy dose of the blues. As with the other highly advanced material excerpted in this book, it's important to remain patient here and work *slowly* through the material, breaking it down measure-by-measure or phrase-by-phrase until each component is under your fingers and can be brought back up to speed and integrated into the whole. The Solo begins with what is sometimes referred to as an *oblique* bend, wherein one string (in this case, the G string) is bent (use your middle finger here) while one or more other strings (B and E here—use your ring finger and pinky) remain stationary. Zakk follows up with a series of two-string oblique bends, finishing off by pinching them into harmonic submission, and then gives us a simple, bluesy phrase in measures 3 and 4. The next two measures are filled with a blisteringly fast tapping lick that you'll want to slow *way* down as you learn and practice it. Wylde doesn't necessarily do a *ton* of tapping, but he's often cited Eddie Van Halen as his favorite guitarist, and a lick like this is an obvious tribute to that master of fingerboard wizardry. Use your pick-hand index finger to tap the higher notes in the phrase while hammering on and pulling off between the index and middle fingers of your fret hand to sound the lower pitches. You'll find that the lower your guitar's action and the more distortion-saturated your tone, the easier the lick will be to play.

In the ninth and tenth measures, Zakk erupts into a quicksilver lick of repeated seven-note groupings played along the top two strings and made up of notes from the D blues scale (D–F–G–A♭–A–C). Again, it's not that the lick is exceptionally hard; it's just exceptionally hard to play at full tempo, so take your time. If you're one of those players who shies away from using the pinky, you're in for a challenge—you'll need that digit to begin the multiple three-note pull-offs. The Solo ends with a 16th note triplet phrase that includes repeated hammer-ons from the index finger to the middle and ring fingers and moves back and forth between the D and G strings before finally ascending to a fevered climax.

TRACK 20   TRACK 21
Slow Demo

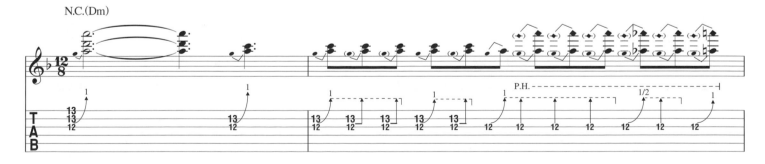

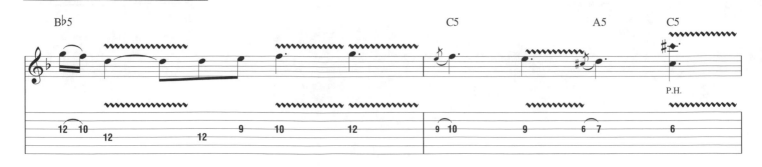

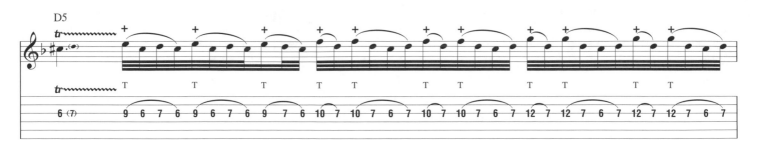

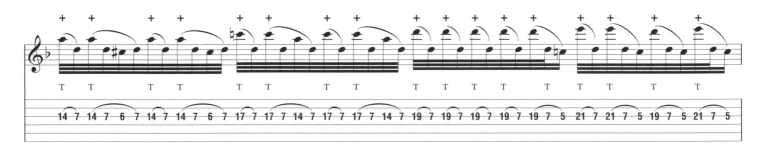

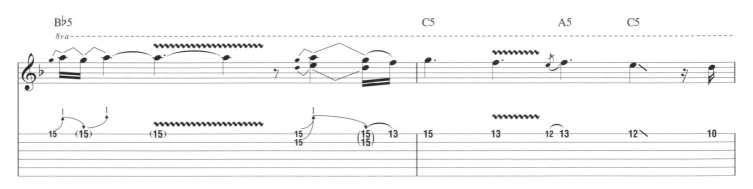

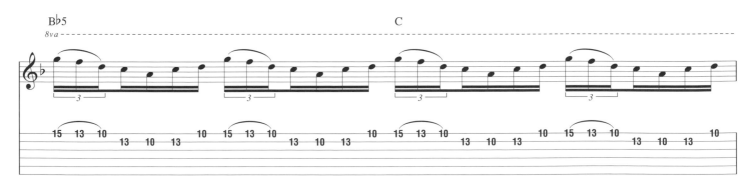

24

1,000,000 Miles Away

from **Book of Shadows** *(1996)*

Words and Music by
Zakk Wylde

One of the traits that separates Zakk Wylde from the pack—and there are many—is his knack for writing truly strong and memorable *songs*. His sense of humor often obscures his very legitimate musical skills, but this is a man with a real sense of melody. His songs aren't just a mish-mosh of cool riffs pieced together or mere launching pads for incendiary soloing, but actual compositions that develop and bring the listener along for the ride. On 1996's *Book of Shadows*, Zakk's first true solo project, he explored material that wouldn't have necessarily been suitable with Ozzy, and a song like "1,000,000 Miles Away," which developed quickly and organically from a studio jam session, had a place to be heard. This one is also a bit different for Zakk in that he used a Gibson SG to record the tune (rather than one of his trusty Les Pauls), a chorus pedal is used extensively, and double-tracking is avoided completely.

Intro Riffs

After a distorted, sustained 10th (the interval between the open low E string and the G at the A string's 10th fret), "1,000,000 Miles Away" hits the ground running with this intriguing Introduction. The material Zakk plays in this section also serves as the basis for the riffs that accompany the song's Verse and much of its Pre-Chorus as well. Play the sliding double stops two measures after the double bar with your index (on the A string) and middle fingers (on the low E). Use the same fingering throughout the excerpt for each of the double stops played on the lowest two strings. Except for a few chromatic passing tones, this section (and much of the song) is based on the E Mixolydian mode (E–F#–G#–A–B–C#–D), the fifth mode in the key of A. This is often used for soloing over dominant chords, as it contains both a major 3rd (G# in this key) and flatted 7th (D). The perfect 4th in the mode (A) also allows Zakk to create a number of suspensions and releases back down to the 3rd both here and throughout the song's Verses.

TRACK 22

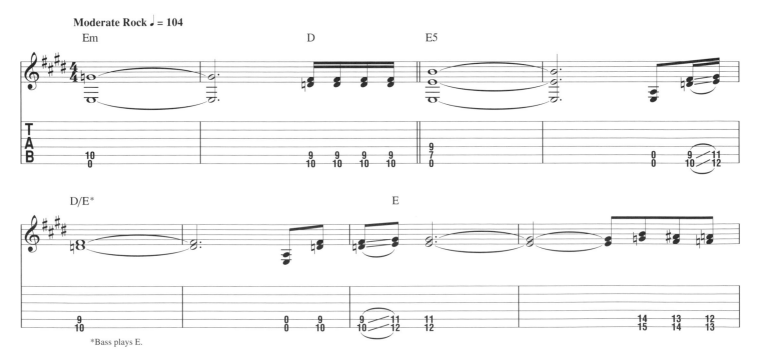

*Bass plays E.

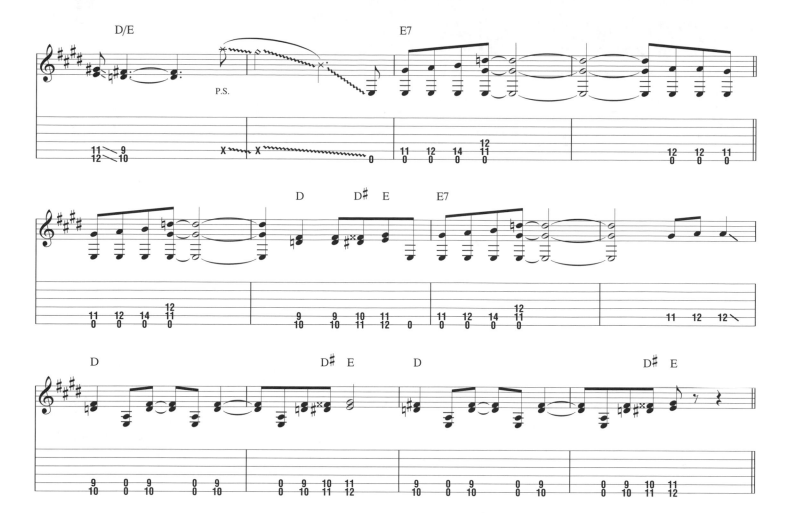

Chorus Excerpt

The Chorus is shown here in a somewhat truncated form, and the eight measures preceding this excerpt are nearly identical to the first four below (played twice). This simple, melodic section is played in a half time feel and moves from Em to G to Cmaj7 and, finally, B7 (the i, III, VI, and V chords in the key of E minor, respectively). We're no longer in Mixolydian territory at this point—we've moved into the realm of E Aeolian (E–F#–G–A–B–C–D), the sixth mode in the key of G. The first four measures of this excerpt involve a bit of faux-fingerpicking—let those open strings ring!—before you stack the tones of a B7 chord up one-by-one and let 'em sustain. Stay in first position here so your middle finger winds up playing the root of the chord (the B at the 2nd fret of the A string) and the rest fall into place above.

TRACK 23

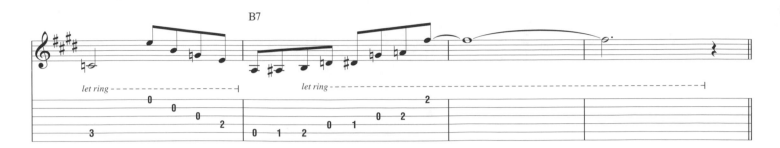

Solo

The 16-measure example shown below includes all of Zakk's Solo played over a loose E minor tonality outlined by the bass (the end of the Solo, in which he plays over the song's Pre-Chorus section, is not shown here). Generally speaking, he's playing mostly from the E blues scale (E–G–A–B♭–B–D) but also includes notes from the E Dorian mode (E–F♯–G–A–B–C♯–D) and hints at the E melodic minor scale (E–F♯–G–A–B–C♯–D♯) in measure 10 and the E Mixolydian mode (see above) in measure 15. The Solo begins with a gradually accelerating trill between the open D string and the E at its 2nd fret that lasts for six beats before releasing into a G-string bend. In an ideal world, we'd all be able to trill equally effectively with each of our fingers, but it's unlikely you'll be as strong with your pinky as you are with your index finger (after some experimentation, I found the middle finger to be most effective here). After repeating the feedback-laden G-string bend, he follows up with a wicked step-and-a-half bend and release on the low E string, then gives us a classic blues repetition lick in measures 5 and 6 (play the bends on the B and G strings with your ring and middle fingers, respectively). There's another tasty bend-and-release in measure 7 in which you'll need to use your pinky to push the A at the high E string's 17th fret up a whole step before bringing it back down and working through a tricky 12th-position lick that includes a number of consecutive Es and Bs. The final four measures of the example feature a long and difficult lick that's as complex rhythmically as it is physically, so take it slow; try learning it beat-by-beat rather than measure-by-measure. Zakk begins with a nine-note grouping and works his way through a series of 32nd notes, sextuplets, and uneven mixed groupings. Be sure you understand these subtle and demanding rhythmic shifts before you try tackling the notes on your axe. For the most part, we're still in blues scale territory, but there are a number of challenging fingering issues beyond the sheer speed of the line. At the end of the first nine-note grouping, you'll need to roll your ring finger to get to the E and A at the D and G string's 14th frets, then roll your index finger to play the B and E on the top two strings' 12th frets. Leave your index finger in place here for the remainder of the measure, as you'll be returning to these 12th-fret pitches often. As the line continues, you shift up to 15th position; use your index finger at the 15th fret and ring finger for the many notes on the 17th frets of the top two strings. There's a pair of pinky bends at the 19th fret near the end of the line, followed by a handful of G♯s that give the lick a temporary dominant 7th flavor before it all concludes with a classic blues lick flourish.

TRACK 24   TRACK 25
Slow Demo

Moderate Rock ♩ = 104
N.C.

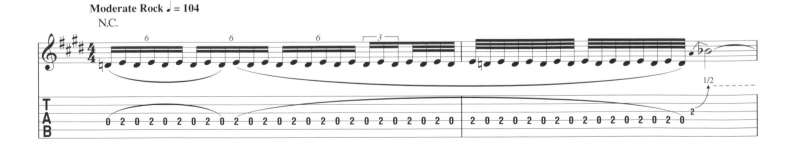

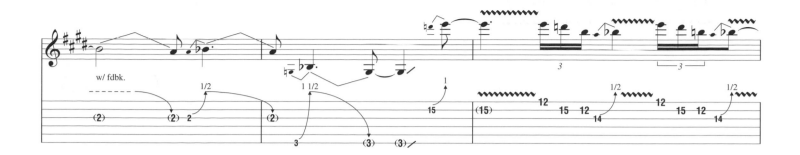

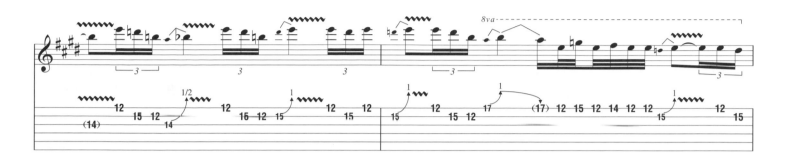

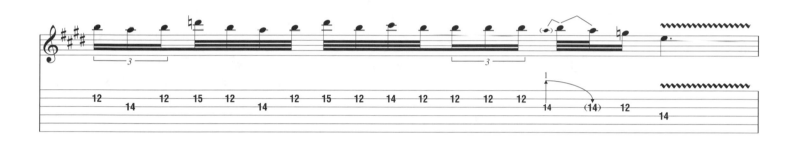

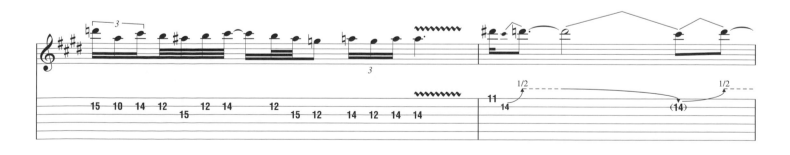

1,000,000 Miles Away *Cont.*

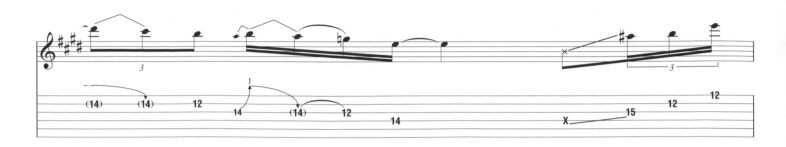

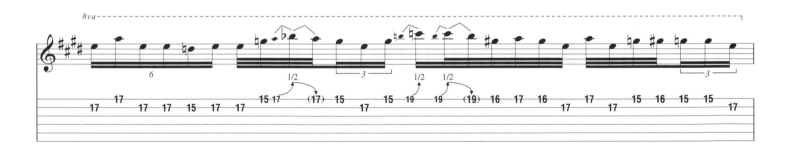

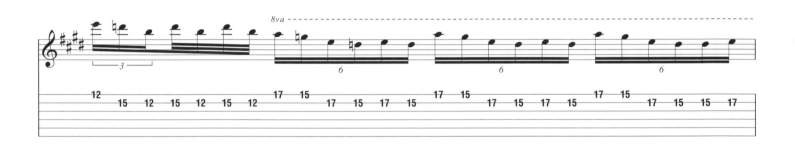

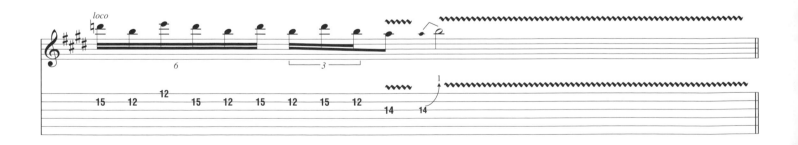

Born to Lose

from *Sonic Brew (1999)*

Words and Music by
Zakk Wylde

The Black Label Society's debut album, *Sonic Brew*, found Zakk Wylde returning to the ultra-heavy, riff-based music fans had come to expect from him. While his work with Pride & Glory and his solo project, *Book of Shadows*, revealed new facets of his musical personality—chicken pickin' country, acoustic instrumentals, and melodic songwriting—BLS was a platform for Zakk's vision of a new kind of heavy metal for the 21st century. "Alcohol Fueled Brewtality" is a sound and an ethic: a beer-fueled, no-holds-barred style devoid of the excesses that had turned the once mighty world of hard rock into a big joke by the late 1980s. BLS didn't have pretty hair and make-up, they didn't use synthesizers, go to movie premieres, date supermodels, or act like prima donnas. This was no-nonsense metal reminiscent of the heyday of the 1970s, when the music's practitioners were grim-faced, unshaven men scaring the crap out of mainstream America.

Opening Riff

At the heart of each of Zakk Wylde's complex and multi-layered songs lie riffs of uncommon power and head-banging ferocity. "Born to Lose," of course, is no exception, and the simple two-measure riff that kicks the song off manages to be funky and tinged with blues feeling while retaining an unmistakable metal vibe. While Zakk has jokingly stated that the Black Label Society doesn't bother with material "you can't play . . . on one string," the opening riff of "Born to Lose" actually employs each of the three lowest strings (doubled an octave lower with a pedal to provide added thickness and depth). Begin the riff by hammering on from your index finger to your ring finger twice; you'll need to shift positions to grab the final two notes in the first measure with your ring and index fingers, respectively. Use your index finger on the 5th fret and ring finger on the 7th fret for each of the notes in the measure that follows.

TRACK 26

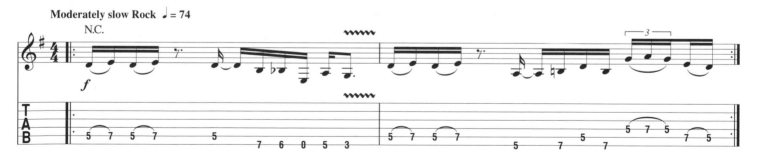

Chorus Riff

Here's the ubiquitous E–to–C progression found in countless metal classics. It's to Zakk's credit that he finds something new and fresh to do with these chords, while making us bang our heads as hard as any of his predecessors ever did. The riff begins with a hammer-on from the index finger to the ring finger that's repeated in every other measure (and in the little grace note in measure 3), and wraps up with some descending octaves along the D and low E strings. This is some of the simplest and most effective music in the book.

TRACK 27

Bridge Riff

Zakk has always been a fan and student of the music of Black Sabbath, and it's reflected in his playing and writing—surely this is part of what has endeared him so deeply to Ozzy Osbourne for all these years. That kind of influence isn't easily abandoned, even when one is trying to do so; this is clear in a tune like "Born to Lose," and in this passage in particular. An abrupt tempo change introduces this galloping triplet lick that's redolent of early Sabbath and feels more like a sincere tribute than a case of mere mimicry. There are more hammer-ons (and pull-offs) between the index and ring fingers here, as well as ring-finger-to-pinky hammer-on and pull-off action along the D string. Maintain an even, alternate picking approach throughout the riff despite the large number of unpicked notes.

TRACK 28

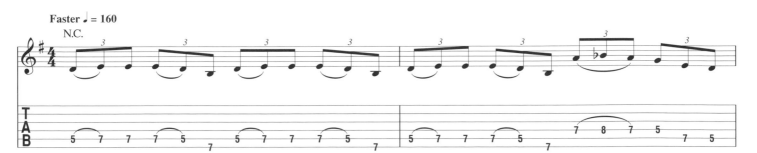

Solo

This is a very atypical Zakk Wylde Solo statement in that it is short, clearly pre-composed, and lacking in runs of blistering speed until the final measures. Even then, the parallel hammer-ons played on the top two strings are (relatively) simple to play, making this a Solo that's easy to learn and accessible to the less experienced player. Begin by using your index finger to bend the D and G strings up a half step, then barre the B and high E strings with your ring finger. The descending trills in measures 3 and 4 (doubled an octave lower via overdub) should be played with the index and ring fingers, and then it's back to more 2nd fret bending. The hammered-on sextuplet phrase near the Solo's end should be played with the 1st, 2nd, and 4th fingers; pick each string once per six-note grouping, then hammer onto the notes that follow (this lick sounds pretty cool in reverse, beginning with a pinky pull-off, as well). Use your ring finger for the final bend, a long push up a step and a half from A to C. Catch the B and G strings as you push towards the ceiling, making for a wild, harmonized bend—it's easier than it sounds!

TRACK 29

TRACK 30
Slow Demo

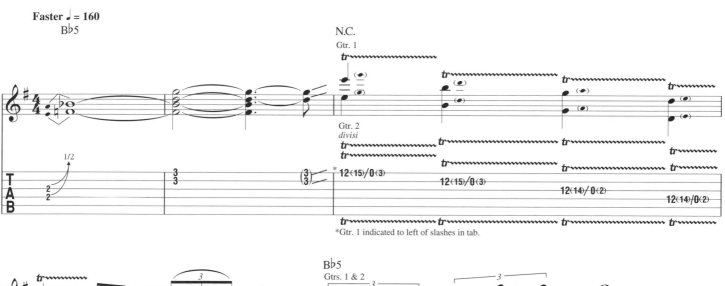

Born to Lose *Cont.*

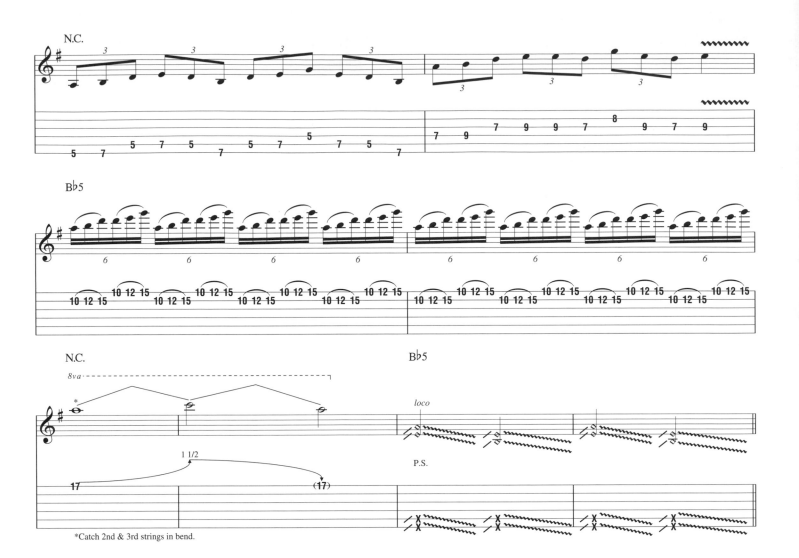

*Catch 2nd & 3rd strings in bend.

Counterfeit God

from *Stronger than Death (2000)*

Written by
Zachary P. Wylde

This incredibly sludgy, medium tempo headbanger from 2000's *Stronger than Death* tackles a subject that's gotten under Zakk Wylde's skin more than once—the hypocrisy and deceit of religious fundamentalists.

Intro and Chorus Riff

After a creepy, backwards-tracked church service serves as an Introduction, "Counterfeit God" gets moving with this heavy-duty riff that also returns during the song's Chorus. Don't forget to lower your low E string a major 6th (!), leaving you with an impossibly low and rumbly G two octaves below your open G string (check your tuning by comparing the two open strings). The part played by Guitars 1 and 2 stays on the detuned low E string until its end, when it's broken up by palm-muted eighth notes on the open A and D strings; begin the part with your index finger at the 10th fret and slide to the 5th fret in the second measure. The slackness of the string will allow you to easily add exaggerated vibrato to the 3rd-fret pick harmonic that follows. Guitars 3 and 4 have a single-note bending line beefed up with an octave pedal; pick only the Gs in the line and bend the string up and down a whole step each time.

TRACK 31

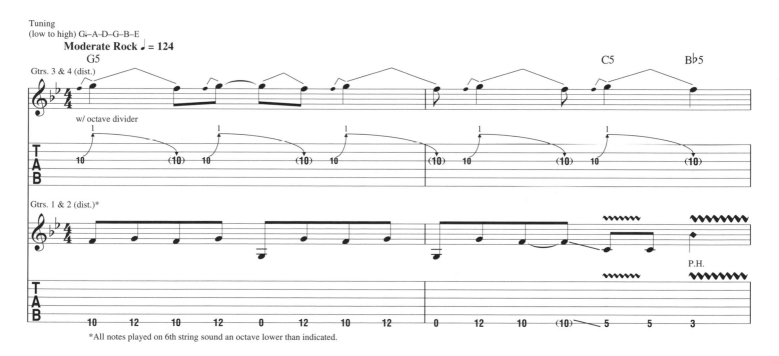

*All notes played on 6th string sound an octave lower than indicated.

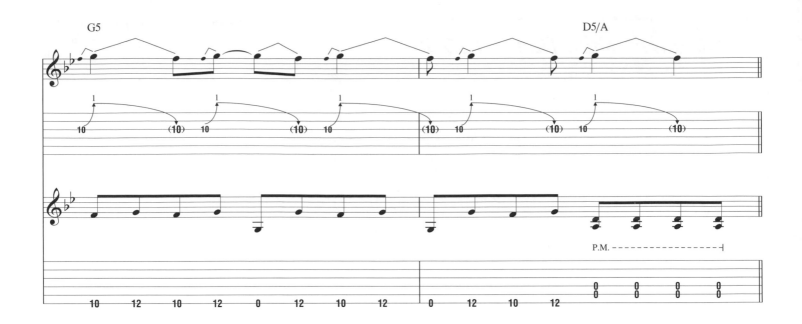

Verse Riff

This simple, bone crunching riff requires only the index finger (for all 3rd- and 5th-fret pitches) and gets its head-banging impact from detailed articulation that includes pick harmonics, wide vibrato, and muted strings. A careful examination of both the recording and transcription is necessary with even the most basic material. Practice the part slowly until you have all of its elements in place—a misplaced palm mute here or there can change the entire impact of the line. Try using all downstrokes for the muted chords to get the proper level of chunk!

TRACK 32

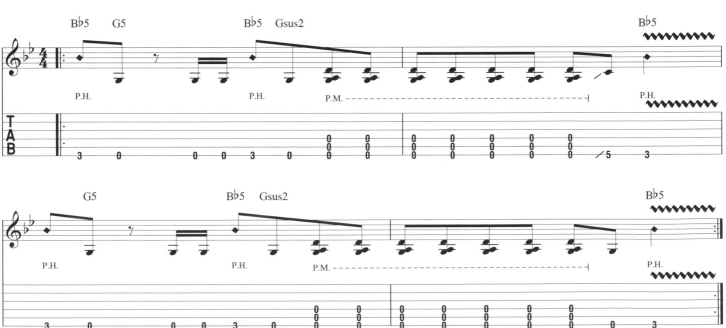

Solo

Zakk doubles himself with a second, overdubbed guitar on this suitably oddball 16-measure Solo. It begins with two measures of trills along the open G string using the ring, middle, and index fingers in the descent. In measure 3, there's a slide up the D string to 15th position for some rapid-fire sextuplet licks built on the G blues scale (G–B♭–C–D♭–D–F) that incorporate a number of tricky repeated notes and pull-offs. Zakk returns to the G-string trills in the measures that follow and employs a nifty right-hand trick: sliding the index finger down the string lightly while trilling to produce a series of harmonic overtones. In measure 9, he returns to the neck's upper regions with a long lick that begins in 12th position before climbing back to the G blues scale in 15th position. Along the way he throws in a few E♮s, lending the lick a Dorian flavor, before spinning off into an unusual chromatic pattern that moves outside of the (loosely) established G harmonic center. The tension is relieved with a quick return to the G blues scale at the end of the lick. There's another oddity near the Solo's end—a triplet-based lick laden with tritones and chromatic passing tones that's purely intervallic and non-harmonic—before a climax is reached with a tremolo-picked F that's gradually bent up a whole step, catching the G string along the way in a frenzy of vibrato.

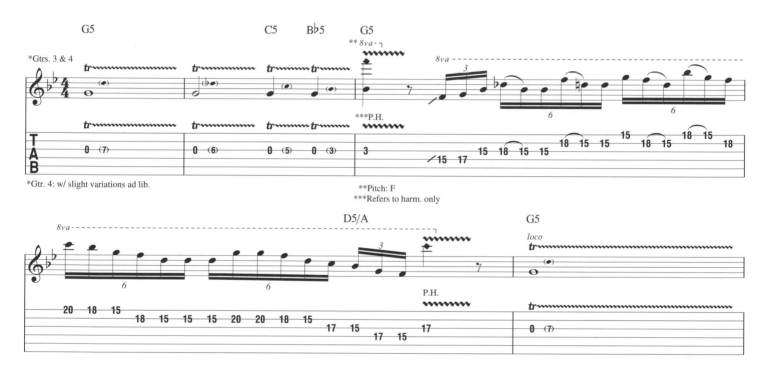

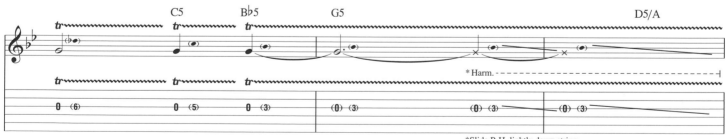

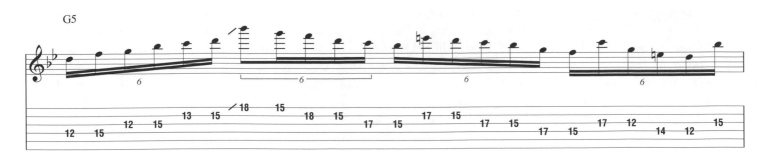

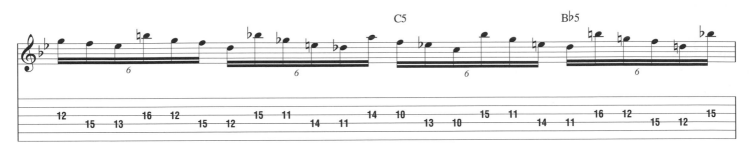

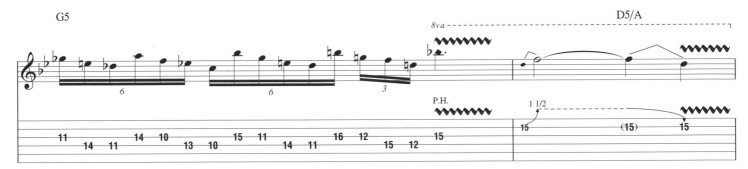

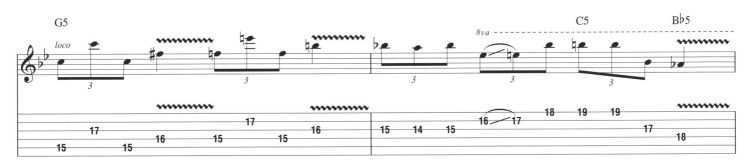

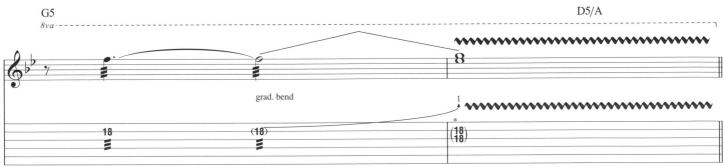

*Note on 3rd string sounded by bend/vib.

All for You

*from **Stronger than Death (2000)***

Written by
Zachary P. Wylde

Copyright © 2000 Bellbottoms and Beer Music (BMI)
All Rights Administered by Reach Global Songs, a division of Reach Global, Inc.
All Rights Reserved   Used by Permission

Here's another medium-tempo headbanger that exemplifies Zakk's no-nonsense, back-to-basics approach with the Black Label Society. All extraneous material has been stripped away, leaving us with a brutal metal masterpiece that feels like a breath of fresh air—and a ray of hope for a once mighty style that was nearly killed off by the 1980s hair bands and the glorified garage rock of the grunge era.

Intro and Chorus Riff

This simple figure opens "All for You" and returns during the Chorus, lending the proceedings a sense of order and cohesion. Zakk drops the low E string down a whole step to D for this song, ratcheting up the heaviness quotient without going completely over the top (as in the drop G insanity of "Counterfeit God"). To play the riff, simply hammer on from your index finger to your ring finger for the 16th note figure on the A string (check out the familiar subdivision employed, in which the measure is broken up into note groupings: three–three–three–three–two–two). The repeated A string riffing is broken up only by a few quick "hits" on the low E, where highly accented pitches are adorned with squealing, vibrato-laden harmonics.

TRACK 35

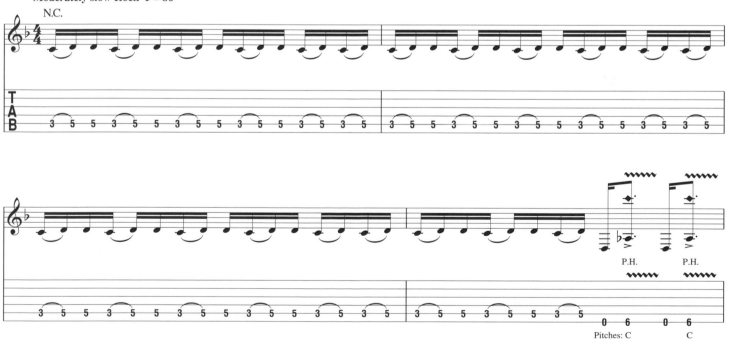

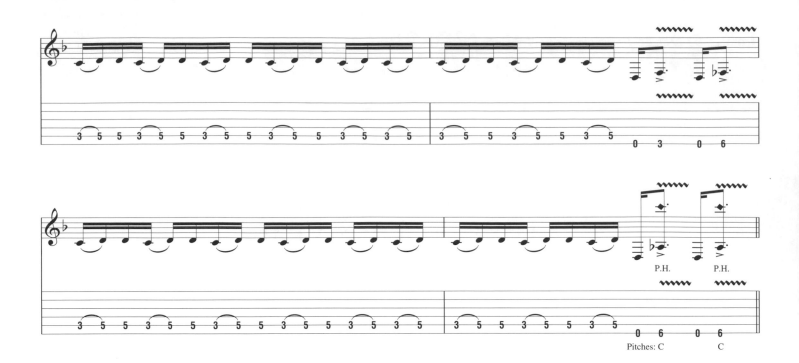

Verse Riff

This two-measure phrase settles into a mean little groove that provides the backdrop for Zakk's heavily Ozzy-influenced vocals. Use your index finger for the 3rd-fret notes and your ring finger for the 5th-fret notes throughout, while observing the palm-muting indications carefully. The line gets a little tricky at the end of the first measure, with a series of descending 32nd notes along the low E string. Be sure you can sing the phrase (or, at the very least, tap out the rhythms on a tabletop) before taking it to your axe. There's a fair amount of anticipation and rhythmic variety here, and a subtlety borne of Zakk's typically detailed phrasing complete with hammer-ons, mutes, harmonics, and the like.

TRACK 36   **TRACK 37**
Slow Demo

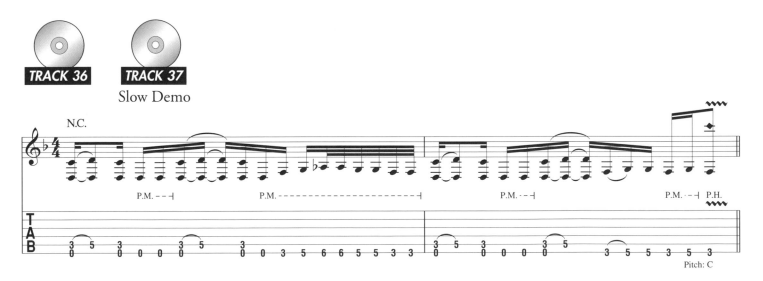

Solo Excerpt

This eight-measure fragment includes the first half of Zakk's Solo, played over a D minor tonal center, taking us up to the point at which the accompaniment shifts to a series of syncopated, descending power chords. Zakk begins by sliding up and down the B string for the first two measures, playing Fs and Es in the low register and following each of these notes with the same pitch an octave above. Try not to overshoot your mark when sliding into the upper register—a task that's easier said than done. After a measure of heavily vibratoed quarter notes and a nifty tapping phrase, he blazes through a handful of quicksilver licks based on the D Dorian mode (D–E–F–G–A–B–C) in 10th position. Use your pinky for each of the 13th-fret notes, with your index finger remaining at the 10th fret for the duration. The more distortion-saturated your tone is here, the better all of the hammer-ons and pull-offs that follow will sound. There are a few nice stretches in the final measure, where you'll have to extend your pinky to the 15th fret to hammer onto and pull off from a high D back to the 10th fret A notes played by your anchoring index finger.

TRACK 38   TRACK 39
Slow Demo

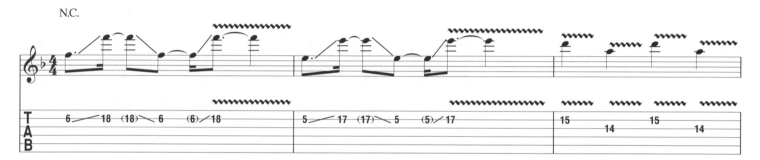

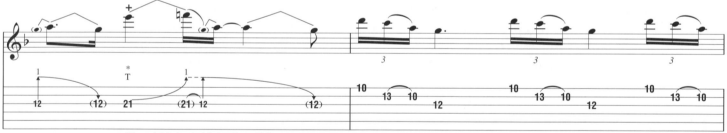

*Tap w/ right hand while bending w/ left.

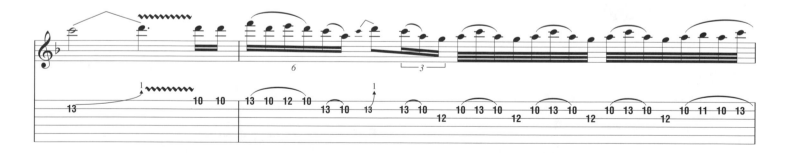

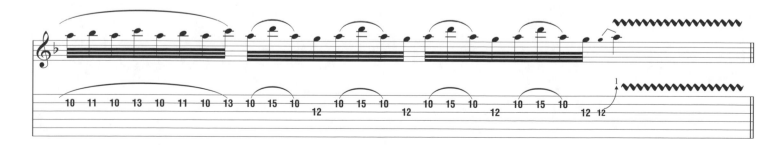

Speedball

from *1919 Eternal (2002)*

Written by
Zachary P. Wylde

Zakk Wylde makes no secret of his admiration for Eddie Van Halen, likely the most technically innovative guitarist of the last three decades. When a journalist showed Zakk the *Rolling Stone* "100 Greatest Guitarists of All Time" issue, in which Van Halen was ranked 70th and Kurt Cobain ranked 12th, the Wylde one nearly went through the roof. Randy Rhoads was ranked 85th, while Joe Satriani, Steve Vai, and Yngwie Malmsteen didn't make the cut at all!

In the end, Zakk was able to laugh it off and get back to the business of guitar, a field in which he's the equivalent of a "Rhoads scholar." With "Speedball," a solo nylon-string acoustic piece, Zakk pays tribute to Van Halen and his classic solo "Spanish Fly," while also nodding in the direction of players like Al Di Meola and Paco De Lucia, fleet-fingered masters whose work has also been an inspiration.

Intro and "A" Section

"Speedball" is shown here in its entirety, broken up into a two-measure Intro, four-measure "A" section with first and second endings, a "B" section with an extended second ending, and a five-measure finale. Be sure to pay attention to the tuning here, and—wait for it—*take your time*. As has been stated before in these pages, this is virtuoso level material that requires a patient approach and a lot of practice (a classical guitar that plays like a Les Paul wouldn't hurt either). Try playing each part perfectly—even at a glacially slow tempo—before you even consider ratcheting up the speed.

The piece begins with a series of sextuplets on descending strings, ending up at the low E and a chord made up of 12th-fret harmonics. The fermata above indicates this chord is to be held for an undetermined length of time. Use your index, middle, and ring fingers on each string throughout the brief Introduction. The "A" section begins after the double bar and continues the sextuplet rhythms of the Intro, this time incorporating hammer-ons and pull-offs that make the job a little easier. The unusual phrase descends in half steps before winding up with a chromatic phrase that descends in parallel fashion until you hit the open E string again. The second ending comes to a clear stop with a highly accented, three-note chord employing the open E, A, and D strings.

TRACK 40   TRACK 41
                Slow Demo

Drop D tuning, down 1/2 step:
(low to high) D♭–A♭–D♭–G♭–B♭–E♭

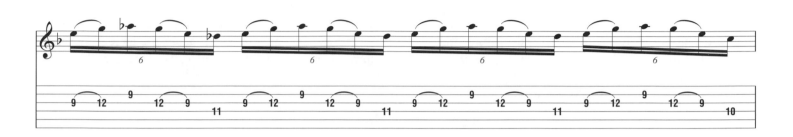

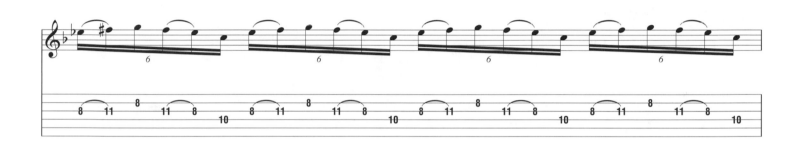

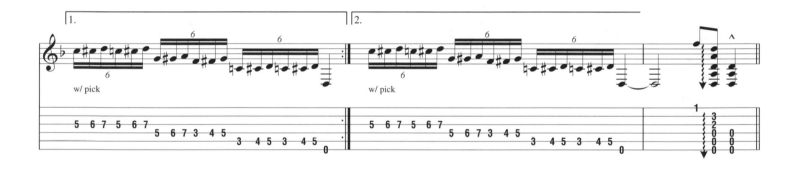

"B" Section

Here's where things get tricky. You'll need to employ a form of hybrid picking throughout this section, picking the B♭ (first fret of the A string) while beginning the pull-offs on the G string by picking with your ring finger. While the B♭ sustains below, revert to the pick for the note on the D string and those that follow. The phrase is repeated in the first measure and then answered by an all-picked phrase that climbs and descends the A, D, and G strings—play these pitches with your left-hand index, middle, and pinky fingers. After a return to the opening phrase, Zakk follows with a lick that includes a series of hammer-ons on the A string contrasted with the open D string. In the second ending, the pick-and-fingers idea is extended, with the roots shifting below while (at first) the upper phrase remains the same. Play the B (2nd fret of the A string) with your index finger, and then pick the open A string while using your index and middle fingers on the D and G strings, respectively. In the final two measures, use your middle finger on the A string while your index and ring fingers get to the notes above.

TRACK 42   **TRACK 43**
Slow Demo

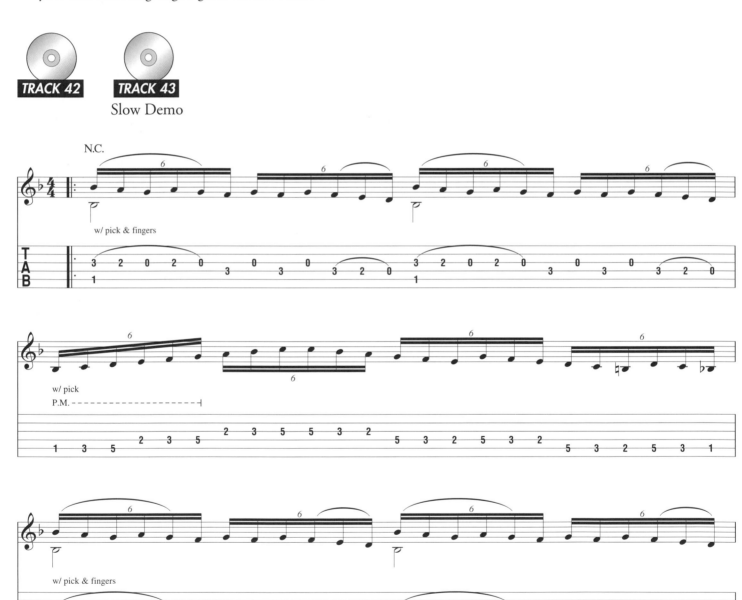

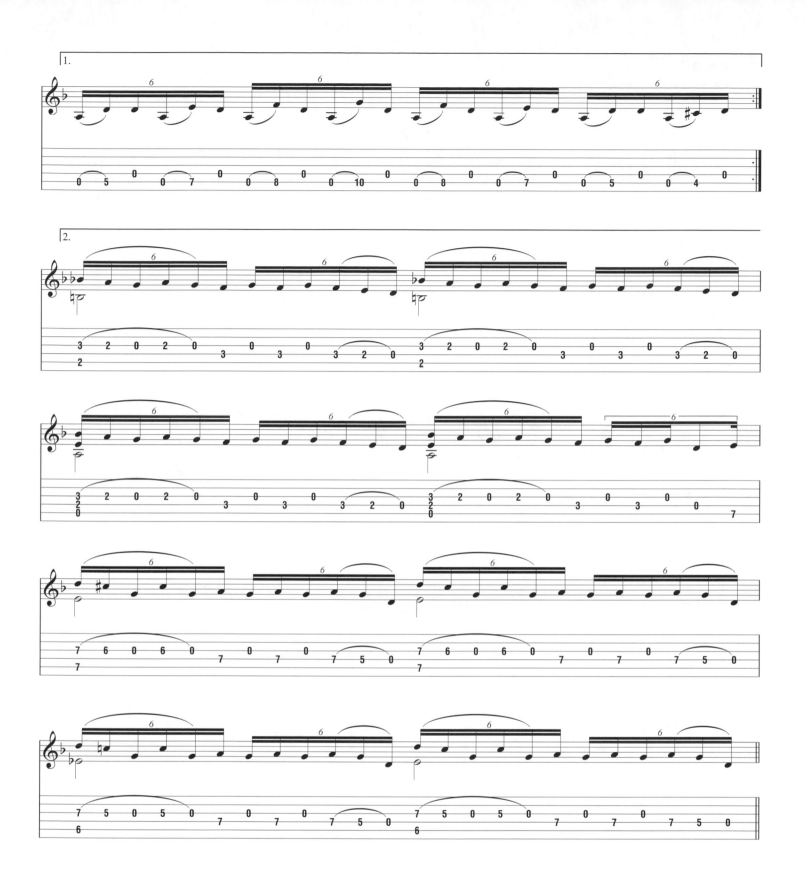

Ending

"Speedball" concludes with a return to the repeated sextuplets that climb and then descend the strings while employing the index, middle, and pinky fingers. Make sure you pick each note here—don't cheat with hammer-ons, as easy as they could make things. You want to develop rapid-fire alternate picking chops, don't you? Here's a good place to put them to the test. After another sustained harmonic chord, Zakk finishes the piece with a descending melodic phrase derived from the G harmonic minor scale (G–A–B♭–C–D–E♭–F♯) that has a Gypsy-ish quality and cadences nicely to an incomplete D major chord.

TRACK 44   TRACK 45
Slow Demo

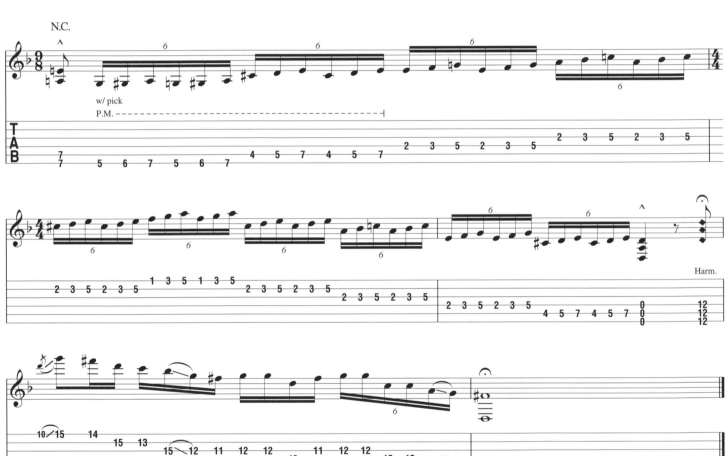

The Blessed Hellride

from *The Blessed Hellride (2003)*

Written by
Zachary P. Wylde

The title track from the Black Label Society's 2003 offering finds Zakk Wylde in a somewhat more pensive mood than usual, but amply demonstrates his ability to sustain a high level of emotional intensity even after the Marshall stacks have been put away. "The Blessed Hellride" also points up Zakk's skill as a composer of memorable melodies and an acoustic guitarist of considerable subtlety and taste.

Verse Accompaniment Pattern

This simple figure opens the tune and provides a *misterioso* backdrop for the Verses that follow. Much of the song's intriguing character can be attributed to its unique harmonic progression that employs chords from both D major and D minor tonal centers. The opening slide from C to Dadd2/4 (use your index finger on the A string and your ring and pinky fingers on the D and B strings, respectively) hints at D Mixolydian (D–E–F♯–G–A–B–C), while the unusual version of the tonic chord includes both the major 3rd and perfect 4th for a distinctly wide-open character. The Fmaj13 and Cadd2/E chords in the second measure are borrowed directly from the D Dorian mode (D–E–F–G–A–B–C) and reinforce the unsettled mood of the tune; play the roots of these chords with your ring and middle fingers, flattening each slightly to mute the unused open A string.

TRACK 46

Drop D tuning:
(low to high) D–A–D–G–B–E

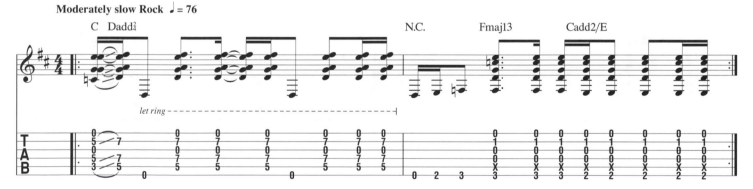

Chorus

The somber mood continues as we move up to Am for the Chorus, continuing the mixed-mode harmonies of the Verse. Both Am as well as the G chords (G5 and G6) that follow are derived from the D Dorian mode, while the D and Dsus4 chords in measures 3 and 4 belong to the D major scale (D–E–F#–G–A–B–C#) or D Mixolydian mode (D–E–F#–G–A–B–C). The section ends by returning to the Verse accompaniment pattern, lending the song a satisfying sense of unity.

TRACK 47

Solo

This unusual eight-measure passage finds Zakk laying down not one, but two rare, clean-toned Solos. The two statements combine to create a lovely counterpoint to each other as they interweave, harmonize, and answer each other's phrases with lines of their own. Try learning each guitar's part as an independent passage, mastering the elements of each before moving on to the next. (This would be a fun one to try with a friend, with each player learning both parts and swapping between them.) Let's examine each part independently, beginning with the bottom line (Guitar 2), the more dominant of the two.

The Solo begins with an oblique bend, in which the C on the B string (use your pinky) remains stationary while the G string is bent up and then released with the ring finger. This short phrase is repeated in measures 3, 5, and 7—a central motif, as it were. There's a simple 16th note phrase in measure 2 built from tones in the D minor pentatonic scale (D–F–G–A–C) played in 10th position. In measure 4, Zakk includes a few G♯s—the "blue" note in the D blues scale— and then brings them back in measure 6 with a lick that ends with a ring-finger slide up the G string to the 14th fret. In the Solo's final measure, he spits out a palm-muted 32nd note line that features repeated pitches moving between the 10th and 12th frets on the lowest four strings.

Guitar 3 (the top line) serves a more subservient role here, answering the phrases of Guitar 2 and filling the spaces with lines of its own. A handful of 16th-fret B string bends are followed by a pentatonic lick in measure 2 that includes a pull-off from the ring finger to the index finger on the G string. The bend in measure 4 (B string, 18th fret) can be played with the pinky or ring finger (try the pinky if you've got enough finger strength), but you'll need to use your ring finger for the 20th-fret bend in measure 5 for a bluesy lick played all the way up in 17th position. The Solo's penultimate phrase moves down to 15th position, while the final lick, a palm-muted descent through the D minor pentatonic scale, is played in 10th position and runs in contrary motion to Guitar 2's ascending line.

TRACK 48   TRACK 49
            Slow Demo

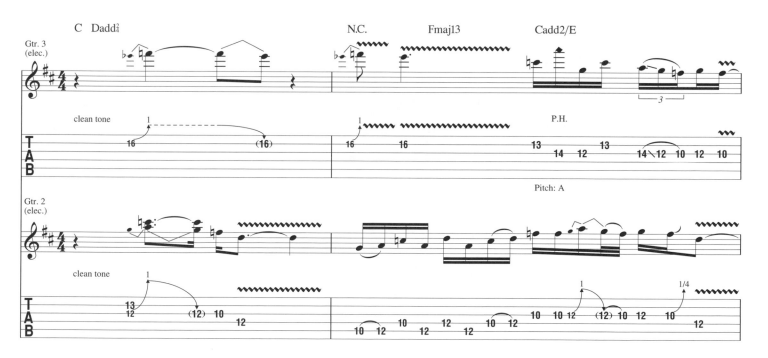

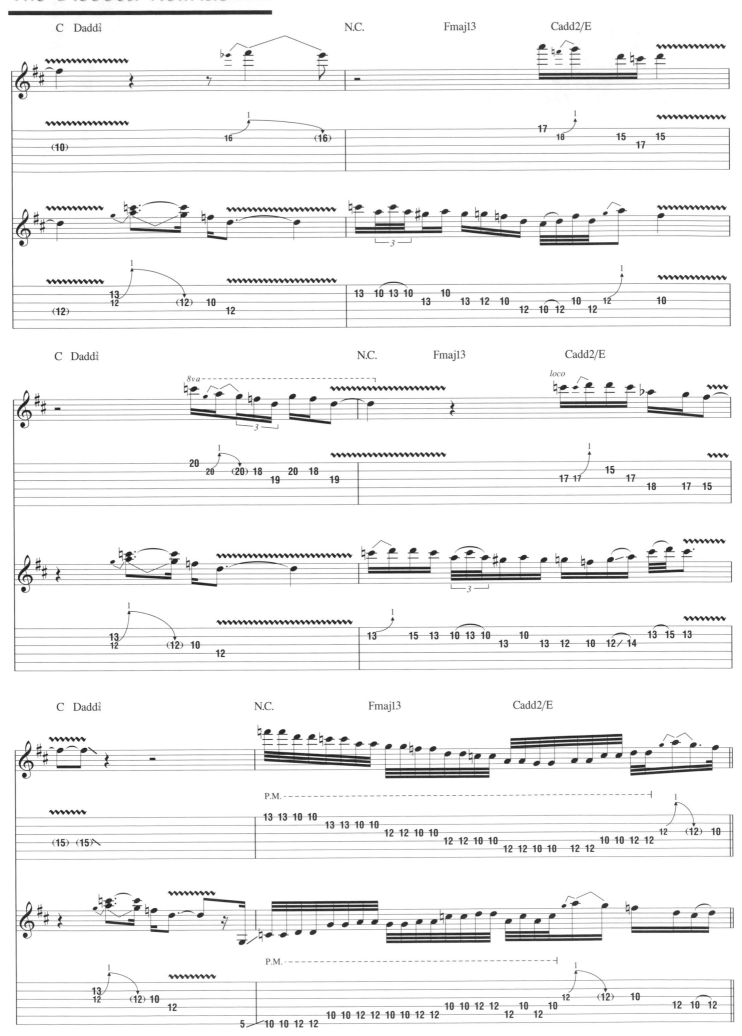

Suffering Overdue

from *The Blessed Hellride (2003)*

Written by
Zachary P. Wylde

Copyright © 2003 Bellbottoms and Beer Music (BMI)
All Rights Administered by Reach Global Songs, a division of Reach Global, Inc.
All Rights Reserved   Used by Permission

The punningly titled "Suffering Overdue" brings to mind the heaviest work of Black Sabbath while updating the metal template with drop tuning and contemporary-styled vocals. The brief, clean-toned arpeggio passage followed by a classic "galloping" triplet riff is right out of the Sabbath mold, but Zakk's furious Solo break demonstrates just how far the technique of today's guitar hero has evolved since Tony Iommi first helped lay the foundation for the next three decades of metal virtuosos.

Intro and Chorus Riff

The drop B tuning employed in this song will leave you with a pretty slack low E string, so you'll have to use a somewhat more delicate touch there to avoid making a complete mess out of things (it'll help if you use an extra heavy gauge string like the .060 and .070 low Es Zakk is fond of). To play this opening riff, pull off to the open A string with your index finger, and then use your ring finger to slide up the low E string to the 12th fret. Each of the pick harmonics in the measures that follow has specific pitches indicated, and it may require a bit of experimentation to accurately match them (try varying the location of your pick attack between your guitar's bridge and the end of the neck to produce higher and lower harmonic tones). Play the last two notes of measures 1, 3, 5, and 7, as well as the grace notes preceding them, with your index finger alone; use your pinky to get to the grace notes and F♯s in each of the measures that follow.

TRACK 50

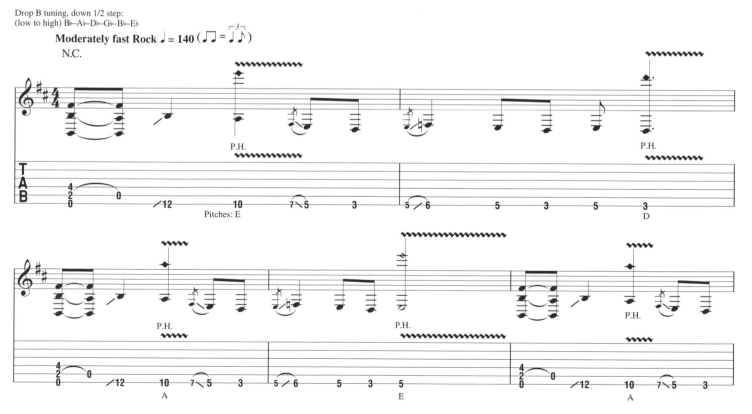

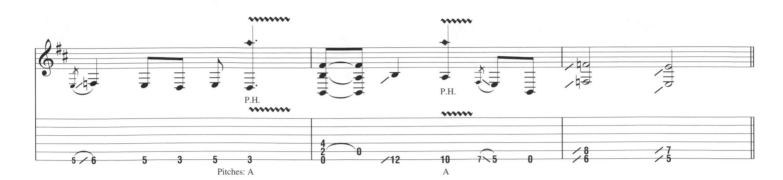

Verse Riff

Heavy metal has always been about one thing above all others—killer riffs—and this mosh-inducing phrase is no exception. It's a simple piece of work, but it's got just the kind of loping, almost swinging rhythmic feel necessary to get the heads-a-banging and the Doc Martens working overtime. Begin with an index- and ring-finger hammer-on to the B5 chord (use your pinky on the D string if you must), and be sure to include each of the carefully placed palm-mutes for greater bone-crunching effect.

TRACK 51

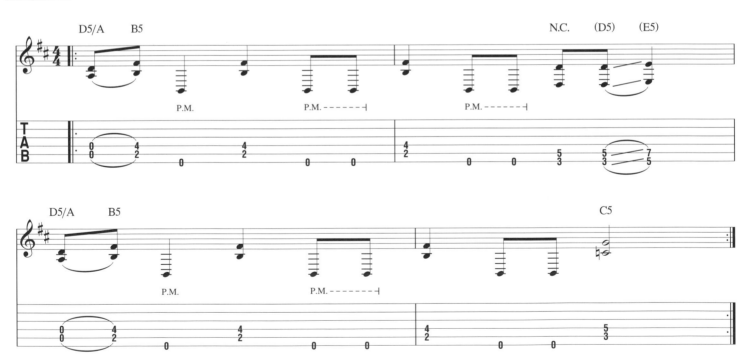

Triplet Riff

This eight-bar phrase serves as a launching pad from the brief arpeggio section to Zakk's wicked Solo. It's reminiscent of Sabbath tunes like "Children of the Grave" and amply illustrates the deep blues influence in that seminal band's music and in the contemporary work of the Black Label Society as well. It's pretty much just a swinging shuffle that's been sped up and dipped in a fresh coat of overdriven tube distortion—and it's in keeping with Zakk's tongue-in-cheek declaration that BLS is only interested in riffs they can play on one string. The pitches are also pretty bluesy—flatted 5ths and the pairing of both major and minor 3rds were the province of the rural bluesman long before they became essential sounds in the metal musician's arsenal.

TRACK 52

Solo

Make no bones about it—this 24-measure Solo is a killer. Zakk begins in 14th position, playing from the B Dorian mode (B–C#–D–E–F#–G#–A) with its distinctive major 6th, as he spits out a fiery lick subdivided into five-note groupings (note the use of the flatted 5th, F♮, as well). There's a quick index-finger slide in measure 4 that brings us down to 12th position before the phrase ends with a blues-inflected combination of minor and major 3rds (D and D#, respectively). The long, repeated sextuplet lick in measures 5, 6, and 7 employs both perfect and flat 5ths pivoting below the tonic (B) and flatted 7th (A). Play the lick with your index and middle fingers on the G string while your ring finger gets the B string above. You'll need to shift quickly later in the line to catch the G on the B string (8th fret) with your index finger. At the end of the phrase, Zakk continues his downshifting by dropping to the 7th position B minor pentatonic scale (B–D–E–F#–A).

He answers a pair of B-string overbends (up a whole step and a half) in measures 9 and 13 with blues scale phrases in 2nd position, then kicks off a long, gradually accelerating phrase in measure 17 that moves back and forth between the top two strings. In the Solo's final measures, he blasts through some 7th-position blues "box" licks, then wraps up by trilling between the 7th and 10th frets on the B string. All in all, the effect is something akin to Eric Clapton after a gallon of Turkish coffee!

Slow Demo

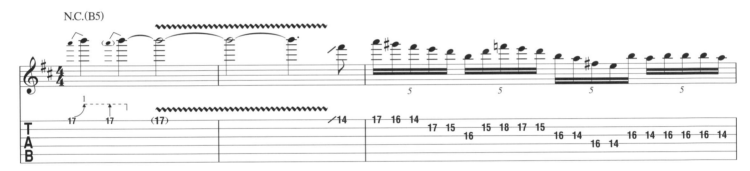

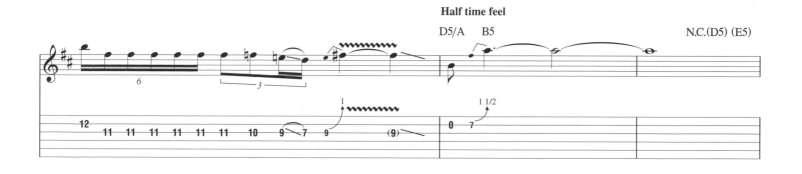

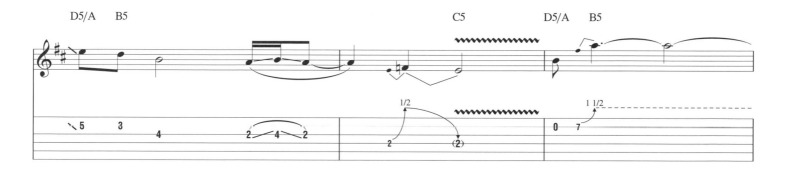

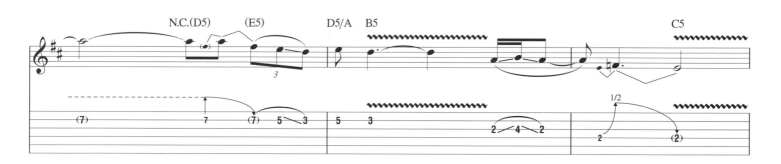

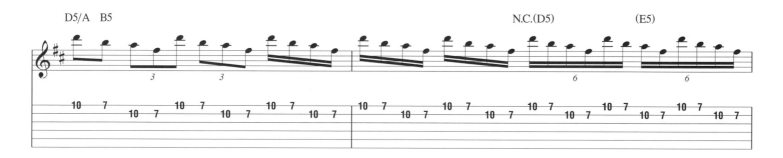

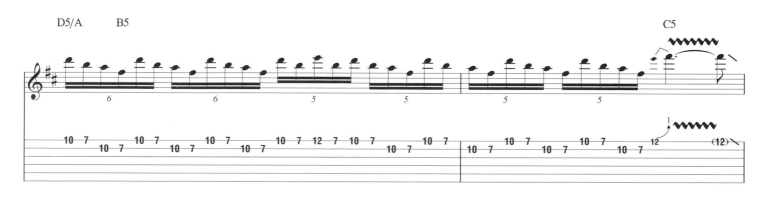

Suffering Overdue Cont.

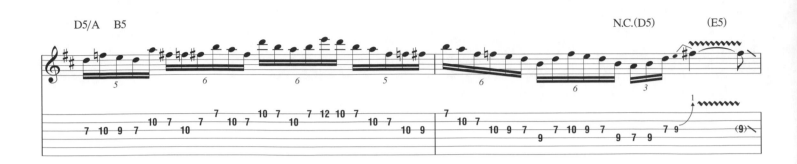

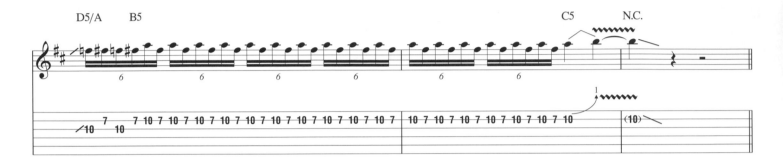

Stillborn

from *The Blessed Hellride (2003)*

Written by
Zachary P. Wylde

This medium-tempo rocker, the final song in our journey through the music of Zakk Wylde, is a simple, melodic composition that would have been right at home in the repertoire of Wylde's long-time bandleader, Ozzy Osbourne. In fact, heavy metal's grand old man *does* lend his vocal talents to the Black Label Society here, putting his inimitable stamp on the song with his distinctive voice while underlining the musical and emotional bond he and Zakk have forged through countless hours in the studio and on the world's most prestigious stages.

Intro/Verse Riff

"Stillborn" kicks off with a single-pitch riff that's simplicity itself. The song's rhythmic base is established while Ozzy lets out a trademark howl that sails hauntingly over the music. As noted below, generate random harmonic overtones by moving your pick back and forth between your guitar's pickups as you "pinch" the low E string ever so slightly.

TRACK 55

Tune down 1/2 step:
(low to high) E♭–A♭–D♭–G♭–B♭–E♭

Moderate Rock ♩ = 108

N.C.(F♯5)

*semi-harm.

sim.

*Create random pinch harmonics by moving
pick between bridge and neck pickups.

Pre-Chorus

The first harmonic change in "Stillborn" shifts us down a whole step to a crunchy, palm-muted E5 chord before returning to the repeated F♯s that form the backbone of the tune. The example below is an excerpt of the Pre-Chorus—its first four measures—and includes one of Zakk's favorite rhythmic devices: over-the-barline phrasing created by uneven groupings of eighth notes. The 16 eighth notes in the first two measures are divided into three- and two-note note groupings followed by a final quarter note, with the beginning of each grouping demarcated by an unmuted double stop on the A and D strings. The effect is especially interesting when contrasted with the steady and even 16th notes that comprise the bulk of the song.

TRACK 56

Chorus

Play both the F#5 chord and the first muted note in this passage with downstrokes, putting you in position to hit the D5 chord with a downstroke as well. To play the sliding octaves in the second measure, use your index finger on the low E string (flattening it slightly to mute the open A string) while getting the notes on the D string with your ring finger. The opening measure of the phrase is then repeated and answered by a stream of palm-muted eighth notes on the open low E string. The section is played twice before releasing into one of Zakk's usual super-shredding Solo spots.

TRACK 57

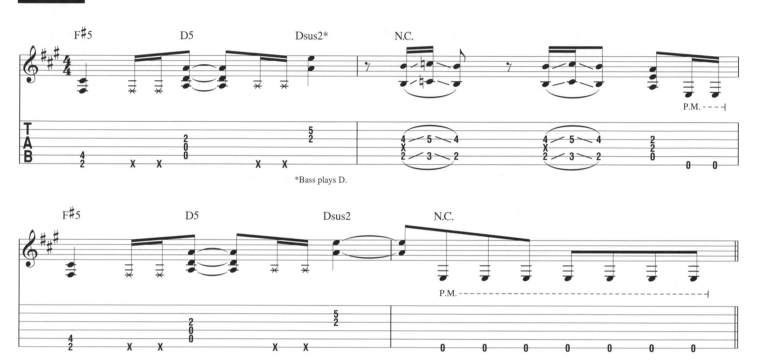

*Bass plays D.

Solo

Like most of the Solos examined in this book, the 12-measure "Stillborn" Solo is doubled with a second, overdubbed guitar, a technique favored by Zakk Wylde and by the metal establishment in general. The presence of a second "voice" adds thickness and dimension to the music, and minute idiosyncrasies of pitch and articulation only serve to strengthen what was already, in this case, a truly wicked piece of work. Zakk gets things started with a long trill (hammer on and pull off rapidly between your ring and index fingers) before sliding up the B string until he leaves the fretboard entirely and runs into the neck pickup. A simple F♯ minor pentatonic (F♯–A–B–C♯–E) phrase follows, including a gradual ring-finger bend on the D string, before Zakk moves up to the 12th fret for a 16th note ascending pentatonic lick. By measure 7, he's comfortably settled into the F♯ minor pentatonic "box" in 14th position and lays down a repeating pull-off and bend phrase on the top two strings (although you *could* use your pinky for both the pull-offs and bends here, most players would be more comfortable employing the ring finger). Zakk continues climbing in measure 8, beginning in 14th position before shifting up quickly to grab a few high As (E string, 17th fret) with his middle finger. Play the B-string whole step bend on beat 3 with your ring finger, and then use the same digit for the measure's final G-string bend at the 21st fret. Measures 9 and 10 include a handful of stock blues licks in second position (bend the G string with your ring finger), while the Solo concludes with a series of accelerating three-note groupings on the top two strings that climb the neck and climax in a vibrato-laden B string bend. They sound (and look) harder than they really are, and if you're playing a guitar with low action and a heavily distorted tone, these three-finger hammer-ons shouldn't prove to be much trouble. Merely pick the first note on each string, and then hammer on from your index finger to your middle finger and pinky as you work your way up the fretboard.

TRACK 58

TRACK 59
Slow Demo

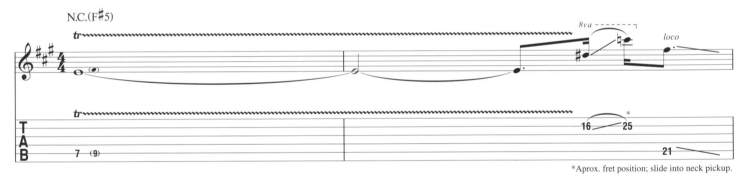

*Aprox. fret position; slide into neck pickup.

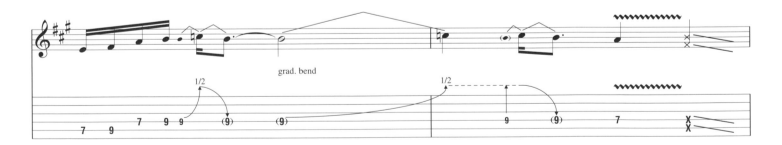

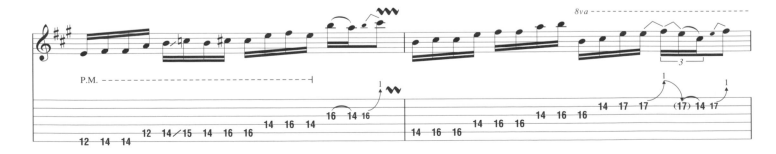

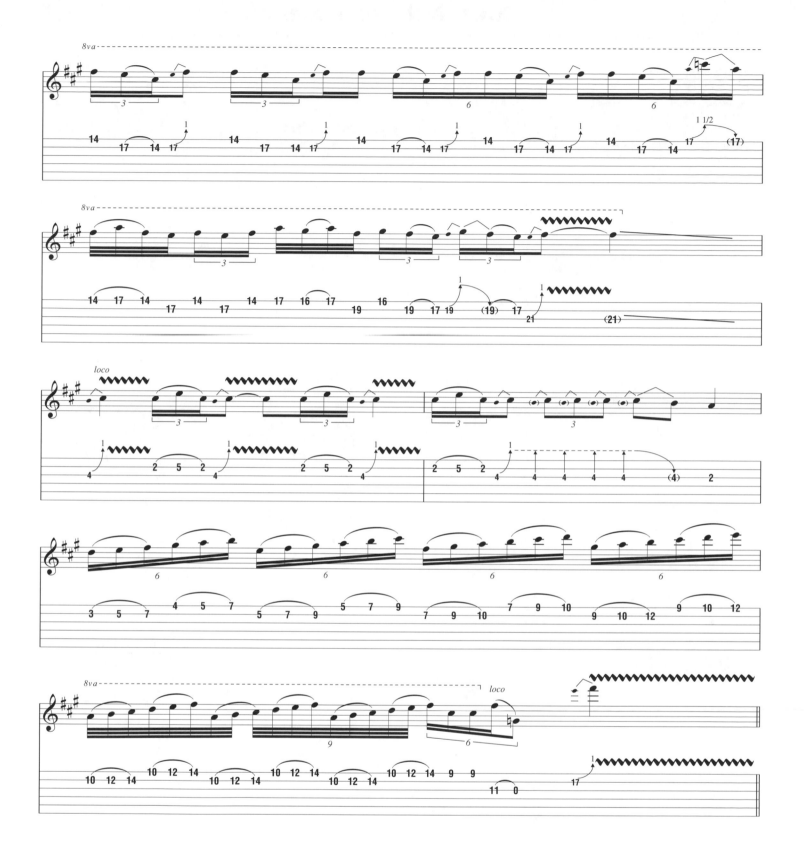

Guitar Notation Legend

Guitar Music can be notated three different ways: on a *musical staff*, in *tablature*, and in *rhythm slashes*.

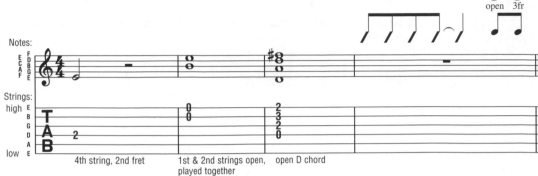

RHYTHM SLASHES are written above the staff. Strum chords in the rhythm indicated. Use the chord diagrams found at the top of the first page of the transcription for the appropriate chord voicings. Round noteheads indicate single notes.

THE MUSICAL STAFF shows pitches and rhythms and is divided by bar lines into measures. Pitches are named after the first seven letters of the alphabet.

TABLATURE graphically represents the guitar fingerboard. Each horizontal line represents a string, and each number represents a fret.

4th string, 2nd fret | 1st & 2nd strings open, played together | open D chord

HALF-STEP BEND: Strike the note and bend up 1/2 step.

WHOLE-STEP BEND: Strike the note and bend up one step.

GRACE NOTE BEND: Strike the note and immediately bend up as indicated.

SLIGHT (MICROTONE) BEND: Strike the note and bend up 1/4 step.

BEND AND RELEASE: Strike the note and bend up as indicated, then release back to the original note. Only the first note is struck.

PRE-BEND: Bend the note as indicated, then strike it.

VIBRATO: The string is vibrated by rapidly bending and releasing the note with the fretting hand.

WIDE VIBRATO: The pitch is varied to a greater degree by vibrating with the fretting hand.

HAMMER-ON: Strike the first (lower) note with one finger, then sound the higher note (on the same string) with another finger by fretting it without picking.

PULL-OFF: Place both fingers on the notes to be sounded. Strike the first note and without picking, pull the finger off to sound the second (lower) note.

LEGATO SLIDE: Strike the first note and then slide the same fret-hand finger up or down to the second note. The second note is not struck.

SHIFT SLIDE: Same as legato slide, except the second note is struck.

TRILL: Very rapidly alternate between the notes indicated by continuously hammering on and pulling off.

TAPPING: Hammer ("tap") the fret indicated with the pick-hand index or middle finger and pull off to the note fretted by the fret hand.

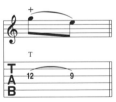

NATURAL HARMONIC: Strike the note while the fret-hand lightly touches the string directly over the fret indicated.

PINCH HARMONIC: The note is fretted normally and a harmonic is produced by adding the edge of the thumb or the tip of the index finger of the pick hand to the normal pick attack.

PICK SCRAPE: The edge of the pick is rubbed down (or up) the string, producing a scratchy sound.

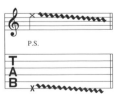

MUFFLED STRINGS: A percussive sound is produced by laying the fret hand across the string(s) without depressing, and striking them with the pick hand.

PALM MUTING: The note is partially muted by the pick hand lightly touching the string(s) just before the bridge.

RAKE: Drag the pick across the strings indicated with a single motion.

TREMOLO PICKING: The note is picked as rapidly and continuously as possible.

VIBRATO BAR DIVE AND RETURN: The pitch of the note or chord is dropped a specified number of steps (in rhythm) then returned to the original pitch.

VIBRATO BAR SCOOP: Depress the bar just before striking the note, then quickly release the bar.

VIBRATO BAR DIP: Strike the note and then immediately drop a specified number of steps, then release back to the original pitch.

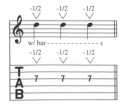

CHERRY LANE MUSIC COMPANY

6 East 32nd Street, New York, NY 10016

Quality in Printed Music

The Magazine You Can Play

Visit the Guitar One web site at **www.guitarone.com**

ACOUSTIC INSTRUMENTALISTS **INCLUDES TAB**

Over 15 transcriptions from legendary artists such as Leo Kottke, John Fahey, Jorma Kaukonen, Chet Atkins, Adrian Legg, Jeff Beck, and more.

02500399 Play-It-Like-It-Is Guitar...........$9.95

THE BEST BASS LINES **INCLUDES TAB**

24 super songs: Bohemian Rhapsody • Celebrity Skin • Crash Into Me • Crazy Train • Glycerine • Money • November Rain • Smoke on the Water • Sweet Child O' Mine • What Would You Say • You're My Flavor • and more.

02500311 Play-It-Like-It-Is Bass $14.95

BLUES TAB **INCLUDES TAB**

14 songs: Boom Boom • Cold Shot • Hide Away • I Can't Quit You Baby • I'm Your Hoochie Coochie Man • In 2 Deep • It Hurts Me Too • Talk to Your Daughter • The Thrill Is Gone • and more.

02500410 Play-It-Like-It-Is Guitar...........$14.95

CLASSIC ROCK TAB **INCLUDES TAB**

15 rock hits: Cat Scratch Fever • Crazy Train • Day Tripper • Hey Joe • Hot Blooded • Start Me Up • We Will Rock You • You Really Got Me • and more.

02500408 Play-It-Like-It-Is Guitar...........$14.95

MODERN ROCK TAB **INCLUDES TAB**

15 of modern rock's best: Are You Gonna Go My Way • Denial • Hanging by a Moment • I Did It • My Hero • Nobody's Real • Rock the Party (Off the Hook) • Shock the Monkey • Slide • Spit It Out • and more.

02500409 Play-It-Like-It-Is Guitar...........$14.95

SIGNATURE SONGS **INCLUDES TAB**

21 artists' trademark hits: Crazy Train (Ozzy Osbourne) • My Generation (The Who) • Smooth (Santana) • Sunshine of Your Love (Cream) • Walk This Way (Aerosmith) • Welcome to the Jungle (Guns N' Roses) • What Would You Say (Dave Matthews Band) • and more.

02500303 Play-It-Like-It-Is Guitar...........$16.95

BASS SECRETS

WHERE TODAY'S BASS STYLISTS GET TO THE BOTTOM LINE
compiled by John Stix
Bass Secrets brings together 48 columns highlighting specific topics – ranging from the technical to the philosophical – from masters such as Stu Hamm, Randy Coven, Tony Franklin and Billy Sheehan. They cover topics including tapping, walking bass lines, soloing, hand positions, harmonics and more. Clearly illustrated with musical examples.

02500100 ....$12.95

CLASSICS ILLUSTRATED

WHERE BACH MEETS ROCK
by Robert Phillips
Classics Illustrated is designed to demonstrate for readers and players the links between rock and classical music. Each of the 30 columns from *Guitar* highlights one musical concept and provides clear examples in both styles of music. This cool book lets you study moving bass lines over stationary chords in the music of Bach and Guns N' Roses, learn the similarities between "Leyenda" and "Diary of a Madman," and much more!

02500101 ....$9.95

GUITAR SECRETS **INCLUDES TAB**

WHERE ROCK'S GUITAR MASTERS SHARE THEIR TRICKS, TIPS & TECHNIQUES
compiled by John Stix
This unique and informative compilation features 42 columns culled from *Guitar* magazine. Readers will discover dozens of techniques and playing tips, and gain practical advice and words of wisdom from guitar masters.

02500099 ....$10.95

IN THE LISTENING ROOM

WHERE ARTISTS CRITIQUE THE MUSIC OF THEIR PEERS
compiled by John Stix
A compilation of 75 columns from *Guitar* magazine, *In the Listening Room* provides a unique opportunity for readers to hear major recording artists remark on the music of their peers. These artists were given no information about what they would hear, and their comments often tell as much about themselves as they do about the music they listened to. Includes candid critiques by music legends like Aerosmith, Jeff Beck, Jack Bruce, Dimebag Darrell, Buddy Guy, Kirk Hammett, Eric Johnson, John McLaughlin, Dave Navarro, Carlos Santana, Joe Satriani, Stevie Ray Vaughan, and many others.

02500097 ....$14.95

Visit Cherry Lane online at **www.cherrylane.com**

LEGENDS OF LEAD GUITAR

THE BEST OF INTERVIEWS: 1995-2000
This is a fascinating compilation of interviews with today's greatest guitarists! From deeply rooted blues giants to the most fearless pioneers, legendary players reveal how they achieve their extraordinary craft.

02500329 ....$14.95

LESSON LAB

This exceptional book/CD pack features more than 20 in-depth lessons. Tackle in detail a variety of pertinent music- and guitar-related subjects, such as scales, chords, theory, guitar technique, songwriting, and much more!

02500330 Book/CD Pack...........$19.95

NOISE & FEEDBACK

THE BEST OF 1995-2000: YOUR QUESTIONS ANSWERED
If you ever wanted to know about a specific guitar lick, trick, technique or effect, this book/CD pack is for you! It features over 70 lessons on composing • computer assistance • education and career advice • equipment • technique • terminology and notation • tunings • and more.

02500328 Book/CD Pack...........$17.95

OPEN EARS

A JOURNEY THROUGH LIFE WITH GUITAR IN HAND
by Steve Morse
In this collection of 50 *Guitar* magazine columns from the mid-'90s on, guitarist Steve Morse sets the story straight about what being a working musician *really* means. He deals out practical advice on: playing with the band, songwriting, recording and equipment, and more, through anecdotes of his hard-knock lessons learned.

02500333 ....$10.95

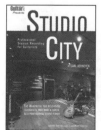

SPOTLIGHT ON STYLE **[CD]**

THE BEST OF 1995-2000: AN EXPLORER'S GUIDE TO GUITAR
This book and CD cover 18 of the world's most popular guitar styles, including: blues guitar • classical guitar • country guitar • funk guitar • jazz guitar • Latin guitar • metal • rockabilly and more!

02500320 Book/CD Pack...........$19.95

STUDIO CITY

PROFESSIONAL SESSION RECORDING FOR GUITARISTS
by Carl Verheyen
In this collection of columns from Guitar Magazine, guitarists will learn how to: exercise studio etiquette and act professionally • acquire, assemble and set up gear for sessions • use the tricks of the trade to become a studio hero • get repeat call-backs • and more.

02500195 ....$9.95

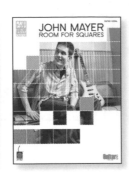